TIMBERDOODLE TALES

Trout Stream Timberdoodle

TIMBERDOODLE TALES

Adventures of a Minnesota Woodcock Hunter

by
Tom F. Waters

illustrated by
Charles J. Johnston

Safari Press, Inc.

P.O. Box 3095, Long Beach, CA 90803-0095, USA

Waters, Tom

ISBN 1-57157-057-8

1996, Long Beach, California

10 9 8 7 6 5 4 3 2 1

Library of Congress Catalog Card Number: 93-84856

DEDICATION

To Roy with memories:

Of painted aspen-covered slopes
and misted pastures,
of blue-and-gold October afternoons,
of creeks and cabins and boys and dogs,
and flashing wings.

ACKNOWLEDGMENTS

One of the greatest pleasures in the production of this book was to work with Charles J. Johnston and Patricia Condon Johnston. Together, with their book-making skills, Charlie's sensitive illustrations, and their appreciation of this remarkable game bird and its habitat, they have guided the production of this small volume into a record of some of my most precious outdoor memories. I am deeply grateful.

It happened long ago, and he may not even remember it, but I am indebted now to Paul G. Heberling, former student and field companion, for the expression, *big, brown butterfly*.

CONTENTS

THE WOODCOCK HUNTER *

A hunter stands at the Pearly Gates,
    a puppy by his side,
And a broken compass dangles
    where his old bandana's tied.
His cuffs and sleeves were badly frayed,
    they were lined with darn and patch.
And some blood ran down a wrinkled ear
    from a recent briar scratch.

"Well, I don't know," St. Peter said.
    "You surely look a fright.
"When most folks climb these Golden Stairs
    they make a neater sight.
"What do you hunt," the Saint then asked,
    "that brought you such travails?
"You must have climbed a hundred hills,
    and walked a thousand trails."

"Woodcock, Sir!" the hunter said,
    "and now and then a grouse.
"But I've always kept my barrels clean,
    and my dog inside the house.
"I've been out on frosty mornings, Sir,
    with my fingers cold and numb,
"Till I couldn't push the safety off,
    with my stiff and frozen thumb."

"I've crawled through brush, and alder swamp,
　　through heat, and mud, and frost,
"But I've never exceeded the legal bag,
　　and never a cripple lost."
Then the hunter presented his setter's name:
　　Old Pete, on a silver bell,
And from an inner pocket, then,
　　a small, brown feather fell.

The hunter took off his blaze-orange cap,
　　and he made his final plea—
"I've been a long-time member, Sir,
　　of the Ruffed Grouse Society!"
By now the Saint was moved to tears,
　　and he shook his snow-white head,
"You looked so bad, I sadly fear,
　　I might have thought you dead."

"How long have you hunted the alder swamps?"
　　he asked, through brimming tears.
"Each season long," the hunter said,
　　"for over fifty years."
"Great Heavens, man!" the Saint exclaimed,
　　"That's surely quite a spell,
"Come on inside, and bring your pup—
　　you've been long enough in Hell!"

*With apologies to poets past.

CHAPTER 1

GHOSTS OF OCTOBER

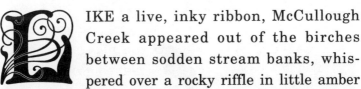IKE a live, inky ribbon, McCullough Creek appeared out of the birches between sodden stream banks, whispered over a rocky riffle in little amber cascades, and then wound down through a misted wooded pasture. Wisps of fog drifted with the current over the water's surface. Alder branches on the edge of the stream were bare and ghostly gray against the black water, but starkly black themselves against a smoky November sky.

And beneath those alder branches not two yards from the stream's edge, locked into a rock-hard point was Spring, my Brittany of eleven years. With her head dipped slightly, she signalled: *woodcock*.

It was late in the season, and a freezing drizzle was ending a gray day, with no woodcock.

From my side, out of sight, Roy whispered urgently, "Give it a try!" The hunting blood came up.

I stepped back at first, swung behind Spring. She held tight. And I edged closer.

This shot, probably, was going to be the last one of my season. The little brown bird, so close but unseen not far from my soggy boots, I knew was prepared to undertake a great journey to escape the deadly cold of a northern Minnesota winter, and to enjoy a sunnier, more salubrious clime. There in those fecund southern swamps it would find the food with which to garner energy for the germ cells that would perpetuate its species next spring.

Here was the ancient moment. My thumb found the safety.

Throughout the history of Mankind's scientific probings into outdoor affairs, perhaps no aspect of natural history has attracted the scholarly efforts of wildlife biologists, or elicited the admiration by hunters and amateur naturalists, as have Earth's great animal migrations: the spectacular vernal-autumnal flights of waterfowl; the eternally moving herds of barren ground caribou; the spawning runs of silver salmon from the sea; even the miniature flights of egg-bearing caddisflies to headwater riffles.

Of these fascinating animal migrations, the mysteries have been largely unraveled.

But the flight details of the American woodcock in eastern North America—southward in October, north again in April—despite mounting interstate and even international research efforts, remain obscure. We have plotted changing abundance through broad geographic zones. Hundreds of thousands of birds have been banded by volunteer off-season hunters and by dedicated biologists. We have even mounted tiny radio transmitters on birds soon to begin their journeys. But essential questions remain unanswered.

Accost some young grouse hunters emerging from one of your favorite coverts, and they may ask: "What were all those little brown birds? They weren't here last week!" Ask a farmer whose ancestors may have pastured the same woodlot for generations, and he might reply: "Woodcock? Well, I don't know. What are they?"

During a single month each year—a mere thirty days—woodcock populations change to such an extent and with such varying amplitude that it seems they must be recapitulating the rise and decline of life on earth. The month, in our part of Minnesota, is October. On October first, if you're lucky, you can find a few local birds; on the fifteenth the autumn swamps may explode with little brown ghosts; and on the thirtieth, most years, they're gone.

The cycle is repeated, with variations, each year.

And it is those variations that give spice to woodcock hunting. The *unpredictableness* of it all. Just as unpredictable, that is, as the weather. For the shape and amplitude of the pattern of woodcock abundance in October is, in fact, tied so closely to the weather of October, and to some extent to that in the preceding September, that the log of an upland hunter's field experience can be taken almost as a virtual weather record.

The very word *October*, to most of us inhabiting these northern climes, is evocative of the bracing glories of autumn-colored coverts under the intense blue of northern skies. Shimmering golden coins on aspen branches all too soon drop their mintage to the forest floor; liquid amber tumbles in the cascades of a northern trout stream. These are the Octobers that woodcock hunters remember.

However, if Octobers everywhere were like those, we might see very few woodcock, indeed.

For it is the cold and storms that start the woodcock down. It is the rain-soaked swamps and moist wooded pastures that keep them here, for a while—it is an extended fall with warm days and cloudy nights that may keep them even longer, sometimes well into November.

Yet the migration itself is inexorable. Given an

exceptionally dry fall, birds seem to trickle through without stopping. An early cold snap in mid-October will rush them through before you're ready. But prepare yourself early in a late fall, and you may wait and wait for "the flight" that never seems to arrive— until it is gone.

Throughout these tales, you might wonder at what may seem to be an excessive concern for the day's weather on a woodcock hunt. Roy and I may have learned to take it as it comes, but still we're sensitive to it. Keep a skeptical ear tuned to media weather forecasts—the very tone of the forecaster may even discourage you from going, and that would be a shame.

When's the best time to go? When you've got the chance, that's when. The weather's all good. In October, that is.

For, about mid-month you may detect a change that's—well—*undetectable:* something in the ground, a surface thickening? You wake up some morning and half the leaves are down? Something in the breeze perhaps? (Can you really smell Canadian air from the northern tundra?)

At night there are more stars than before, and you notice the first wraiths of frost along alder swamps. The sliver of a new moon catches your eye one night, in a sky as black as a timberdoodle's eye: this is the woodcock moon, Burton Spiller tells us. It calls down the legions of little brown ghosts that, he explains, will follow its silvery light right through all his favorite coverts.

So don't wish for every October day to be one of cloudless sky and dry trails.

Wish first for the rains of September. Pray for a few wet days in early October when warm, soaking drizzles renew the soil's essential juices of life, and up north cold snaps bluster and bestir ancient migratory instincts. Then hope for a night when the northern front will drive the clouds away, to reveal the woodcock moon in all its silver splendor.

Then, next day, tramp the spreading, bosky valleys. Follow your pointer or spaniel through a wooded pasture splashed with the crimson of maple. Pick your way up the shimmering course of an aspen-lined trout stream, through your blue-and-gold October day.

For soon enough the northern cold snaps will descend closer and closer. From a distant southern Gulf, warm swamps will call their silent siren notes to these little brown followers of the seasons, and soon, like all ghosts, they too will be gone.

No, you will not see one of the grand spectacles of natural history here—no strings of southward-wandering hooved mammals stretching from horizon to horizon, no noisy wavering echelons of birds against windy skies. You'll have no warning from those reporters who keep track of such goings-on. But ramble down a rural road at dusk in autumn and you'll see them, fluttering shadows against a darkening western sky.

And take two or three one morning, if your shooting eye is sharp enough, from a favorite creek-side covert in front of your pointing dog. And the next morning you'll find two or three more, appearing as if from a conjurer's wand.

And if you're lucky and miss one or two, you may see a flushed bird swing unalterably toward the south—before it disappears.

You will have witnessed all there is to see of the autumn migration of the American woodcock.

The brown ghost came hurtling up through bare alder branches, as neat as could be, from in front of Spring's nose. The bird dodged one branch as I tried to track it. Then another. Stumbling back and forth as I cursed the twisting clumsiness I was making of myself, I just couldn't get it off.

With tight lips I watched the fluttering form grow smaller in a darkening western sky, veer off to the side, and disappear. Indeed, it seemed to turn off to the south.

Then I relaxed. A warm feeling crawled up my back.

Aha! I thought. Beautiful—perfect! The last woodcock, probably, in the whole of Spruce County, and I was there to watch it fly off into southern shadows, without even firing a shot.

I chuckled at my good fortune.

"Tough break"! Roy called out.

But I knew he was grinning like Alice's cat.

Now why would I have gone and shot the last woodcock in the whole of Spruce County?

CHAPTER 2

THE FIRST WOODCOCK

ET me try to explain that.

Take the first time this thirteen-year-old stepped into his uncle's autumn-colored woodlot with a shotgun in hand—after squirrels.

"Pick out two or three den trees," Old Jim the barber had told me. "Sit down on a stump and wait."

How did Old Jim know that just the right arrangement of den trees and sitting stumps was to be found? Of course, it worked out that way.

And when a big fox squirrel stuck his head out from a crotch high in the big dead red oak, I was sure that Old Jim had been there before.

High against a brilliant October sky, the squirrel bobbed around the dead limbs, orange tail flashing and looking huge. I stood up on the stump.

My chest had been about to explode. But at the time the only thing that mattered was that big squirrel that was still alive and might still get away, and the mechanics of the ancient sixteen double I held in my arms.

No marksman, either on the tournament field or in jungle war, ever looked down the length of a gun barrel with greater intensity. And when the sixteen's right barrel roared, the squirrel disappeared from his big blue sky, with one last flash of orange tail.

Both the squirrel and I hit the ground—the squirrel from his lofty height and me from the rear side of my stump. Not at the same time, of course, because the squirrel had farther to go. I must have bounced, more or less, and then with heart stopped, fearful—and hopeful—I swept a panic swath through fallen leaves to the base of the big oak to retrieve my prey.

I didn't do much more hunting that day. Not seriously anyway. The weight of the squirrel, fat and heavy as he was, made a constant presence, and I couldn't concentrate well on other den trees or sitting stumps. I circled around the woodlot a bit, not able to sit and wait for more than a few minutes before I was up, practicing what I was going to say about the squirrel when I got home, and how I was going to describe the action to a friend. So I shot at no more squirrels, and I headed home.

On the way back to my uncle's farmhouse I walked along the edge of the trees, not paying much attention, feeling back often to make sure the squirrel was still there. The edge of the woodlot dipped down into a small swale, the trees dropped away on all sides, and small brush and grass increased. I encountered a blowdown, a big dead elm, and I stepped past some brush that I learned to identify only many years later—a clump of speckled alder.

I wasn't ready for more game. And certainly not for the manner in which it soon presented itself to me. But when I stepped under a leaning limb, the world suddenly exploded.

Up from the vicinity of my feet came a big, brown butterfly, and it seemed as if the alders rattled and shook, as it made its way through alder limbs and dry leaves and, leveling off, bore away to the side and into the shadows of the woodlot.

I didn't bring my gun up. I don't believe I even thought about it. I stepped back, shook up a little.

Vaguely I recognized it as a woodcock. I'd read about them in *Outdoor Life,* seen pictures, heard Old

Jim and some of the old boys talking about woodcock in the shop. But I didn't know much else. Why was that one here? Were there more, deeper in the woods perhaps? I had no guidelines like den trees and sitting stumps.

I did no more feeling to see if the squirrel was still in my coat pocket on the rest of the walk back. And somehow all the fine narrative about my squirrel kill, that I'd practiced back in the woods, just never got said the same way when I sat at the supper table that night.

Congratulations on the squirrel had been in order when Dad came home from work. After supper he helped me clean it. And when the mess was over, still down in the basement, I suddenly blurted out:

"I saw a woodcock, too, at the edge of the woods."

I wasn't sure he was going to believe me. But he stopped short, looked at me closely, and our eyes met, somehow differently than ever before.

"What did you do?"

"Nothing. Should I have shot? Is the season open?"

I thought his eyes twinkled, just a little.

"Season's open," he said, gravely. But it seemed he was grinning, too, inwardly, just a little.

That was my first woodcock, and it must have been

something like three years or so until there was the second.

In the meantime, I hunted squirrels and rabbits with a reckless abandon. Sometimes at night, before a planned hunt, I couldn't get to sleep for the hundreds of squirrels and cottontails bouncing through my insomniac images.

I tried baseball in high school, but the trout season came along and the green infield and white uniforms were forgotten in favor of green woods and white water. In the fall, there was football, but that only lasted until the opening of the squirrel season.

I couldn't get enough gunsmoke in my nostrils. Looking back, this early predatory period still somewhat surprises me. Man's old instinct for the chase, I suppose. I don't understand it, and I won't argue about it.

But over the years the instinct changed, although it never disappears. The first real change came all at once. It required another bright October day—and a familiar clump of alders.

I had hunted my uncle's woodlot many times after that first squirrel. And many times I had passed the wooded edge with the alder clump. It must have grown larger in those years, but I probably didn't notice, because I put on a foot or so myself. A few times I had actually walked through the little thicket with the express idea of finding the woodcock again, once even in the middle of winter when my jacket bulged with cottontails. And never any woodcock.

But this time it was different. It was mid-October; winter still was far around the corner. And there was a certain feel to the woods, to the look of the little depression with the alders, to the day's weather.

I can only suppose, now, that it was the same kind of day because it was the same time in the season, the same point in woodcock life history. I stopped at the edge of the opening, and peered into the shadowed brush as if knowing that its hidden mysteries must by the force of my will be revealed.

And I stepped forward into the alders. I had never shot at a flying bird before, yet I watched the alder branches rather than the ground. And when the bird got up, it was like an old film played over again.

He jumped from a spot under the alders that could not have been as much as a yard removed from where he flushed three years ago.

The image of the rising bird in front of me seemed awesome, as it still does today. It rattled up through the alder limbs, leveled, swung toward the woods. And at my shot it pitched over, wheeled right into the ground. It didn't fold—there was no puff of feathers—it just pitched into the forest floor.

Of course, I thought—or hoped—it was hit. I approached the spot where it had come down, cautiously, peering at the ground, for I knew it would be difficult to see. And then I saw it—apparently in full life, bright eyes shining, feathers unruffled—an occurrence (spotting a live woodcock on the ground) that only very rarely happened to me later. I was sure it must be wounded.

Now, had this been an injured squirrel or rabbit, or even a grouse, I think, I would immediately have raised the old sixteen-gauge to shoot again and stuff the carcass in my jacket. But not now. Not with this strange new prey.

I took one more step, and the woodcock bolted again. I was struck dumb with disappointment.

It was in the main woods now. It flew low and seemingly very fast. It was a wheeling, quartering flight through yellow foliage, the kind of flight I was to miss many times in later years.

It was my own slowness, I suppose, that helped that time. For by the time I got the shot off, the bird had leveled out in an opening of sorts, and it was straight-away.

All the way back to my uncle's house I held the little brown body in my hands. I stroked its feathers, peered into the bright black eyes, estimated the length of the bill and took note of the little hook at the end. Across the long open stubble field to the barn, the squirrels in my jacket seemed tremendously heavy.

That evening, after the dressing and washing chores were done with in the basement, I took the cleaned squirrels and woodcock up to the kitchen. I had the woodcock in a separate pan, and it was that pan I took to stand beside my mother to show, with great expectations.

When she clucked, "My, it's awfully small, isn't it?" I was offended.

And in the harsh, superior tones of developing youth, I informed her of such things as skill and sportsmanship, arguments I had never used before, or even thought of, yet which now somehow became my position of long standing.

It was a watershed. No more did hundreds of bouncing squirrels and cottontails fill my dreams.

Instead, gray alder branches etched the scarlet woods and blue sky and, one after another, in my reeling brain were the rising and fluttering of big, brown butterflies, each with a long grotesque bill that sported a little hook on the end.

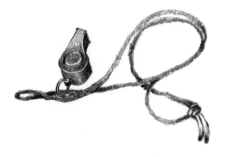

CHAPTER 3

McCULLOUGH'S PASTURE

HE next year I received my introduction to pointing dogs and some hunting ethics—and to McCullough's pasture.

It was the fall of 1941, and I was a junior in high school. A nephew of Old Jim the barber—Ed, his name was—came in from out of town to spend a few days. He stayed with Old Jim while he was there, and Jim got us together one afternoon in the barber shop. Ed had brought with him a little English setter, and he said he knew John McCullough and his woods.

McCullough's woods was not much to look at from the road. That, of course, was in its favor. It was really a pasture, for John McCullough ran cattle in it, and though it seemed like pretty slim pickings for cows, it turned out to be one of the choicest pieces of woodcock cover I ever came to know.

From the road, it was just thick brush, flat, monotonous, uninviting. But back a ways there were little swales, sometimes with water, lined with alders. There were rolling little ridges with blackberry and bracken and hazel, although McCullough was always trying to get rid of the bracken as he said it was poisonous for the cows. There were clumps of birch, scattered aspen, occasional patches of small red oak. And what we came to call McCullough Creek.

The cows were never a problem, and I don't think I ever seriously bothered them either. But John McCullough put them in the woods once in a while, and apparently it was just enough. Looking back now, I realize that he was engaging in management of classic woodcock habitat.

Ed and his little setter stayed in town for a week, including the two weekends. For me, it was a week of wonder and excitement, of bird magic. We hunted every day, except one maybe, and at least for part of each day we were in McCullough's pasture. On the first Saturday and Sunday, we were out all day, and on the weekdays Ed would hunt the mornings alone and then pick me up at the high school door in mid-afternoon.

A little overweight, Ed was, I guess, gray headed. He carried a beat-up, old black pipe and smoked it just once in a while. He didn't talk much, but I learned quickly to listen when he did. And he grinned a lot.

The first Saturday I did a lot of missing, and Ed did a lot of grinning. We didn't see many birds—not like later, anyway—but I guess Ed and I were sort of getting acquainted. Getting used to the dog, too, was something I had to do. Several times I stepped up behind her, at Ed's direction, jumped when the bird jumped, and repeatedly got all fouled up with thrashing arms and alder branches and exploding gun. In mid-afternoon I got one, in front of a perfect point, out in the open, a good clean kill. The grin on Ed's face that time was a fine reward, and a feeling of self-satisfaction rushed up through me as if I had just walked out of a cold winter day into a warm kitchen.

I don't remember all the woodcock that week. They seemed to increase in numbers as the days went on. And there were a few grouse, too. The first one I got I shot off a tree limb, after one had jumped up from the dog and sat peering down at her. When I shot, the grouse fell flapping and the dog rushed in. I glanced at Ed for the usual grin of approval. But there was none, and I shot at no more sitting grouse that week.

When Ed picked me up on the second Saturday morning, the day before our last day, he said, "There's a big storm up north. The flight's really in."

There was no storm here, but rather it was a golden day. A little wind, not much. And there seemed to be a woodcock under every alder. The English setter just went from one point to another. The northern storm must have literally rolled waves of birds down on top of previous waves.

Ed didn't do much shooting. He timed his shots so he didn't get too far ahead of me, and we finished up the woodcock cover together. We hunted out the afternoon looking for grouse, Ed got a couple, and we called it a day. When we walked back to the car in McCullough's farmyard the sky was clouded, a wind was up, and fine driving snow was beginning to fill the air.

I rode home in a perfect trance; I had found a treasure trove that seemed inexhaustible, a find of beauty and exhilaration that would be a driving force in the rest of my life.

The next day should have been an anticlimax, and it was. When Ed picked me up on Sunday, there was an inch of new snow on the ground, and the temperature was below freezing. The wind was still up, and the broken sky of white and blue patches was moving fast overhead.

"There may not be many today," Ed had said, but I didn't believe him. Not until we had tramped through the cold and wind for a couple of hours— without seeing a woodcock—did I fully comprehend that the bounty of birds, there yesterday, were gone today. We flushed a couple of grouse that went out wild in the wind, and missed, and quit at noon.

In the car, with our burning cheeks and freezing fingers and steaming coffee, Ed said, "It was a good week, my friend, one of the best. They're gone now, until next year."

I didn't say much going home, I guess I didn't even say thanks to him like I should have. I was numb and feeling dumb. And not only from the trudge in the freezing wind, but still from the week of days filled with a pointing setter and wildly fluttering woodcock, now in the midst of the frozen white landscape seeming so improbable.

Ed never came back to McCullough's woods.

I looked forward to him during the next year, hoping for a repeat of the past season. But when I asked Old Jim about him one day in late summer, Jim said that Ed, an old chief engineer in the navy, had been called back to help shake down a new destroyer. I got a letter once, a year later, from somewhere in the South Pacific. He'd been thinking about how the woodcock migration was this year, he wrote, and would I keep an eye on McCullough's pasture?

In the big record book of memorable woodcock days, McCullough's pasture stands out twice more for me. One, like my own introduction to the cover, was a

first: fresh and new, full of wonder and mistakes. The
other was an ending, poignant and glorious, like an
October sunset.

It was many years later, and I had had Spring for
ten or so of those years. Danny was just twelve and
had his first shotgun, a single twenty-gauge.

He had started out with some firearm safety
instruction in the Boy Scouts, did some plinking with
his troop, and we'd been out with the clay birds. He
hit the targets well; so well, in fact, that I guess he
acquired some over-confidence, and I know I did, too,
for I was already counting his probable bag.

Spring had been in peak form for many years,
mature, seasoned, an aging veteran.

John McCullough was an old man now, and a son
about my age was running the farm. He still pastured it lightly, occasionally cut a few of the larger
trees out. Danny, Spring, and I drove out on a day off
from school, late in September. The day was overcast,
humid to the point of being a little hazy, with a very
light breeze.

It's a bit of a walk from McCullough's barnyard
to the woods, across a cultivated field and some pasture with willow-lined marsh. By the time the three
of us had crossed, the hunting blood was up. I could
see already the flush, the flight, the burst of feathers,
hear the echo of the little twenty-gauge.

Danny was husky for his age, tough-legged, a
good hiker. His big brown eyes were confident, yet
full of anticipation. And after only five minutes in the

woods, Spring eased into a perfect point in a small patch of scrubby oak, on a rise at the end of a small marsh. Danny eased up just as nicely alongside her.

That time he didn't get the safety off. Another five minutes, and he managed to get a shot off at a second bird, but late, and he missed.

Two good points. And though we had no birds yet, I felt good. Already, I mused, he's had the experience of seeing the dog work and woodcock flush.

A little farther in we stepped down into a patch of alders. Spring froze, just where I expected her to, and when Danny stepped in, two birds bolted up.

"Take yours!" I shouted. He shot, missed, and I downed the other. Spring retrieved it while Danny watched, brought it to me. He watched with wide eyes, and I thought: Now he's seen a good retrieve.

Though early in the season, there were plenty of birds. Almost immediately Spring found another, and Danny missed that one as the bird disappeared over the far edge of the alders.

"Try to get on 'em a little quicker," I suggested.

In the next half-hour Spring made two more good points. Danny shot at both, missed both. Feeling frustrated, I picked off one of those with a long shot.

We worked quite a while, then another point. Danny missed again. Chagrined, I said, "Well, we'll get you one yet."

I stepped out ahead, but he hung back, a strange look on his face. Discouraged, I thought.

Then he blurted out, like a great pronouncement,

"I'm out of shells."

I was dumbfounded, unbelieving. Out of shells!

"How many did you bring?"

"Six," he said.

It was a perfect woodcock day. Good weather, plenty of birds, Spring working with precision. I saw it all going down the drain, for I shot a twelve.

"Well, the limit's five"—he swallowed—"and I brought one extra."

I picked up one more woodcock, and a grouse that jumped from the edge of a grassy pothole, on the long, long walk back to McCullough's barnyard.

Danny did eventually get his first woodcock that season. And though it was not in McCullough's woods, the next couple years saw him sharpen his shooting eye there to the point of great precision. We trudged over every inch of McCullough's pasture, through the alder patches and around the potholes and ridges and along the creek. The little twenty-gauge barked in every corner of the wooded pasture, and eventually it seemed to literally rain woodcock when he went along. And he began to pick off a few grouse, too.

Each time, I noticed, he started out weighted down with a full box of shells—at least.

There came a day in late October one year, and I went

out to McCullough's woods for a sentimental hunt. Just me and Spring. Sentimental, that is, because I didn't really expect to get any birds.

Spring had hunted all season so far, but it was slow going. I was breaking in a new Brittany that year, too—Speck. And all season long, with both dogs along, it was a matter of two extremes. The pup would scramble around Spring, circling, occasionally flushing a bird. Spring padded in front of me, pointing, retrieving, stopping often. Soon the pup got the idea of the point, and when Spring froze quietly on a bird, Speck would ease up behind, flash point, and often jump into the bird. It was obvious that it was high time I concentrated on the pup's training, and just as obvious that Spring should work alone, if at all.

The foliage was pretty well down when we went out, only a few of the oaks still retaining their dry leaves. The sun was bright, but with little warmth. A light frost was on the ground, and the slick, black, muddy patches in the field we crossed to the woods were crunchy. That walk was longer than usual, and I helped Spring through the fences.

Into the edge of the woods we stopped and rested, but not long. Spring sensed the hunt, and while the old legs trembled, her eyes were bright.

We hadn't gone far, no more than five minutes, when she eased into a point. I slipped up behind her, a woodcock flushed, and I dropped it. It was not far away, and she had it spotted, and she padded ahead and found it immediately. She showed no sign of slowness as she brought it back. And then she was out again, ahead of me into a thin patch of hazel and young birch.

Almost immediately she stopped, frozen to a point. But it was a weak point, unsteady. She peered back at me once, and I thought: *a grouse.*

But when I stepped beside her, the brown bombshell went up, and I dropped that one, feeling good as the bird plummeted down among the hazel limbs.

When Spring padded forward for the retrieve I had a feeling that things weren't right. It was farther out this time, and I didn't think she had seen it fall. I stayed back, biting my lip, mentally pushing the dog out, praying that she would find it right away.

She didn't. And I worried some more, watching her search for a few minutes, and then I walked up toward her.

And then, off to one side, twenty feet from her, almost soundlessly, a woodcock rose and fluttered up, through to the top of the hazel brush and silently away in the scattered patches of sun. I didn't shoot.

A sick, heavy weight slipped onto my shoulders. As sometimes happens, a woodcock will plummet groundward at a shot, from the shock of the sound, probably, only to flush again when it is found. That bird, I knew, was not hit.

I kicked myself for missing. What a hell of a way to end it!

Whether Spring saw the bird get up or not, I don't know. It seemed she didn't, for she continued to

search and probe the ground. I whistled, but she
didn't come. I walked toward her to pull her off the
old scent. But then I stopped, for she had, too—on
point!

Maybe! I thought, biting my lip. *Just maybe!*

I stayed put, waiting, hoping.

And she broke the point, took another two
padding steps, nuzzled into some grass at the end of a
deadfall, and came up with a bird in her mouth. She
headed back toward me, her eyes finding mine.

I flushed, and felt like bawling.

She came all the way to me, put the little brown
form in my hand as I knelt, and then she lay down,
settling into the dry leaves on the ground. The other
bird, then, was a third one, now far away. But neither
Spring nor I were thinking of that one.

For a brief moment the idea flashed in my head
that we might have a big day; the birds were really in.

But when I stood up, she stayed down. I broke
my gun then, put the parts in my jacket, and picked
her up.

That was a long walk back, too. And when we
reached the station wagon, I turned with her to look
across to the wooded pasture. I hoped she could see
the birch clumps, the hazel and alder runs along the
edge, the dry oak leaves now rustling in a breeze, and
all the invisible woodcock that must be there.

For I couldn't see a thing.

I carried her to the wagon, and to her blanket in
the back.

CHAPTER 4

THE ALDER CREEK CHAPEL

 HAT came to be known as our Chapel Cover I found while on an early search for land for our family cabin. (I did most of this searching in the fall.)

Carol and I had wanted a place along a river; most vacation cabins in Minnesota are lake places, crowded together in regular shore communities. We wanted more space, more scene than a flat expanse of water out the front window, more solitude in varied topography. Besides, this kind of land, especially with marsh, swamp, or creek, was cheaper. And besides that, there were other considerations—like woodcock cover.

Now, Alder Creek runs down north to south almost through the entire length of Spruce County. About in midcourse, where it might even be called a river in our country, a minor county highway crosses it. At that point, its valley is wide and brushy, stream banks lined by narrow strips of dense alder. On one side, next to the alder, there used to be a large, grassy meadow. A few old apple trees on a small rise and a crumbled stone foundation gave testimony to a long-ago farmstead. It looked more like sharptail country, and I stopped there one early fall afternoon.

I parked in the meadow, and Spring and I made our way upstream along the banks, picking through the alders. I don't remember how many woodcock we found that first day. Not many as I recall, but I do remember that each one flew across the stream to the cover on the other side. Over there I saw thicker cover—not heavily wooded, but aspen saplings, a bright splash here and there of young red maple, hazel clumps and dogwood growing up. It apparently had never been put to the plow, but obviously it had been cut over. That day I didn't have time to explore it, but I remembered it.

When Roy and I pored over some topographic maps of the county, searching for possible cover, I pointed it out. Along the county road on the wooded side, a tiny clearing showed on the map along with a symbol for a building—and the words "Alder Creek Chapel." We hadn't remembered it, though we must have previously driven past it.

So later that fall, we stopped the wagon in the "chapel" yard. No longer used for Sunday services, the building seemed somewhat in disrepair, but it had the look of an early church or school. Since the grass surrounding it was kept reasonably trimmed, we guessed it was now used as a township hall. Back of the structure was the woodlot I had observed from across the creek, comprising some larger trees, mostly oak, probably left standing at the last timber cutting.

So, from the county highway neither side of the stream looked like much for woodcock cover, and it never did seem to attract much attention from other hunters. Across the county highway from the meadow, Alder Creek entered a large, mature woods, heavily posted. With deliberate intrigue, we parked in the old meadow, walked on the road across the bridge to the chapel side and, when no cars were visible, quickly slipped into the woods behind the old church.

Immediately we broke through the larger trees, and ahead, stretching as far as we could see, was the long strip of cutover I had seen from the other side, a hundred yards or so wide, gently sloping down toward the stream. It was as I remembered it—gray dogwood and hazel, scattered alder clumps, small maples now bare, and at the bottom of the slope a dense strip of alder next to the water. We didn't go fifty feet before Spring snapped into a point in mid-stride. Roy took the flush, dropped the woodcock neatly up ahead. And after Spring retrieved the bird to me and I tossed it to Roy, we looked at each other, grinned, and chuckled till we both were nearly laughing.

Up ahead lay a quarter mile of the cutover slope, under a clear blue northern sky. That day the birds accumulated quite satisfactorily in our vest pockets.

We occasionally hunted the narrow alder strip on the meadow side, and birds were there, too. But mostly it was in back of the chapel where we found the first of many secret coverts, and a day of roaming around Spruce County frequently ended—or started—at the chapel.

One year, a severe drought lay upon the upper Midwest country all summer and fall. It wasn't broken until late heavy rains came almost at the beginning of winter. So many of our usual spots were powder-dry during the bird season, and our favorite pastures held no soils moist enough for earthworms or woodcock.

But along Alder Creek in back of the chapel, strips of alder sometimes no more than a few yards wide held almost unbelievable numbers of birds. It was tough shooting in the thick alder, and most birds, it seemed, simply flushed low and flew across the stream. We didn't shoot at these; Spring had always hated to cross water or retrieve a floating bird.

But most years it was not the dense alder strips that held the most birds. It was that moist cutover slope in back of the chapel, unseen from the road, with its brush and saplings and young forest, that provided the greatest of bird hunting for the two of us.

After ten years, the young forest changed. Saplings grew to trees, the slope no longer received the low westering sunlight, and woodcock, on their flight south, no longer stopped there in the former numbers we once knew. But those were ten years of glory—the autumn days filled with the sound of Alder Creek's riffles, scenes of amber water and blue sky, and crimson maples on the slope. And pointing dogs and swift flushes.

And thus we conducted services on many a bright Sunday morning.

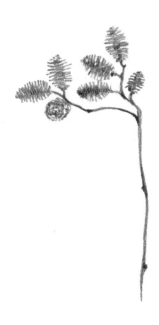

CHAPTER 5

THE SCHOOL TRUST
FORTY

ACK when town and section lines were first laid out in our part of the country, some foresighted fathers set aside sections 16 and 36 in each township as dedicated properties for the support of local schools.

These lands were to be held in trust by the state, later to be judiciously sold at public auction, as the need for school funds arose. All this, of course, transpired after the original white pine had been cut by the lumber barons and the land deemed worthless

anyway. The choicest of the parcels—those blessed
with high-and-dry sites for farm buildings and homes,
or flatlands potentially tillable—went first.

What were left over—creek bottoms, marsh,
alder swamps, slopes of hazel brush and rotting pine
stumps—remained in state ownership and open, of
course, to public hunting.

All the aspiring bird hunter needed for an amaz-
ing guide to some of Spruce County's choicest bird
coverts was a plat book with the state properties in
sections 16 and 36 marked out on each township.
Which little matter, of course, Roy and I took care of
early on.

The parcel making up our forty in question was
legally designated as the SE1/4 SE1/4 Sec 36 of
Thistle Township, Spruce County. Much of the other
six hundred acres of this section had long ago been
sold to private owners, and on either side of the forty
were some abandoned fields (still graced by a deserted
farmhouse) and a Christmas tree farm, respectively,
neither posted. A dirt township road ran along the
south side of the forty, and to the north of it, inaccessi-
ble by road, lay many hundreds of acres in tax-forfeit
status. And down through the middle of the school
trust forty, in its lower reaches, flowed Alder Creek.

I suppose the first time Roy and I hunted it, it
was the best. At least it was the most *different* kind
of woodcock hunting we ever had. As I recall (with
some uncertainty, because it was a fair time ago), we
didn't bag very many, although I guess we should

have.

But I'm getting too far ahead. Before understanding just why these Alder Creek bottoms were so productive of woodcock, we should try to unravel some of the geological history of this little part of Minnesota.

Alder Creek is one of about a half-dozen small streams that flow approximately parallel to each other, arising on top of a low range of hills known locally as the Danbry Mountains (officially as the Backley Moraine), and running only about twenty miles or so until they all empty into the St. Croix River. The Backley Moraine ranges northeast-southwest, and these streams all flow at right angles from it, that is, to the southeast. Below the moraine, the terrain flattens out to a sandy outwash plain, and here Alder Creek, after tumbling down the side of the moraine in rocky riffles, slows considerably.

A few thousand years ago, I'd guess, the creek had slowed enough on this sandy plain so as to form extremely meandering loops, with the wide, sweeping bends almost touching back on each other. Later, it seems, something happened to increase the gradient of the stream—perhaps an uplift of land—and many of the old meanders were cut across.

Today, Alder Creek flows fairly straight in this area—leaving literally dozens of shallow, muddy, curving oxbows slightly elevated above the present stream. The shallow valley, barely a quarter-mile wide, now consists of a flat bottom filled with the oxbows scattered amongst brushy low ridges covered with hazel, prickly ash, and some scrubby oak. It's tough going, tougher shooting—and, in season, full of woodcock.

But after a wet summer, the old oxbows remain full of water—you can't navigate the bottoms at all without webbed feet. And after a couple years' dry spell, the oxbows are empty and dry but covered with marsh grass, good for nothing except swamp rabbits.

Under one special set of circumstances, however, the shooting is remarkably open and easy. Those special circumstances that existed the first time we hunted it for woodcock were, I think, something like this: The oxbows were filled with water in the spring and early summer; this prevented the growth of grass and other plants. Then in late summer a dry spell caused the water to evaporate, except for the remainder of small pools. And each oxbow was left with moist, muddy flats around all sides, bare of almost all vegetation.

And on each of these mud flats, on that early November day long ago, around each curving oxbow were two or three woodcock.

One morning, we slowed the wagon coming down the road's sandy slope, cautiously crossed a rattly wooden bridge, and stopped, plat book in hand.

"This is it," Roy said, and tossed the book into the back of the wagon.

I turned off the ignition. Out the window, on Roy's side, I could see crudely lettered signs nailed to assorted trees and old fence posts promising shooting, death, and dismemberment to trespassers. But that was on the south side, Section 1 of the next township below. Out my side there were no signs. Just brush. And oak trees. Unlikely for woodcock, I thought.

Now, this was a time when I had Spring. She was still young, four years old—maybe five, just hitting her real prime. She had become reconciled to the requirement of retrieving woodcock—up to a point. In the previous season, she would only bring one out of the brush (by a wing tip), lay it down in sight of me, and then wander off pretending she knew nothing of it. But this year she had been bringing them to my feet, if not to hand. It was the beginning of a half-dozen superb years.

This day was near the end of the season—cool, sunny, windless, leaves down.

We got out of the wagon.

Spring, released like a steel coil from the back seat, circled the wagon three times before we had the door shut, then she wandered off to the bridge and down the bank for water. Roy and I loaded up.

It wasn't the appearance of the brush and trees along the road that attracted us, for that kind of cover didn't look anything like the alder edges and open pastures we had become used to in Spruce County. Rather, I think, it was simply the fact that this was a piece of Section 36; it was a piece of land that no one else wanted, for anything. And, of course, there was Alder Creek. We were used to that.

So we left the sandy road, jumped the ditch, elbowed our way through a line of prickly ash and under oak branches—and stopped to eye our first encounter with a mud-lined oxbow.

"I'll go around this side," I said to Roy. "I'll meet you at the other end."

Roy agreed. And he didn't take more than three steps until a woodcock fluttered from his feet, rose into the lower branches of an oak, and flew on ahead out of sight. Roy didn't shoot.

"Where was he?" I inquired.

"Damfino," Roy replied. "There's nothing in front of me but *mud!*"

"Maybe he was digging worms in that mud," I joked.

Roy laughed. Just a little.

Then I took three steps around my side of the oxbow, and a bird got up in similar fashion. I at least got off a shot, but did not connect.

"Where was he?" Roy demanded, now on the other side of the oxbow.

"In the mud again," I said. And Roy laughed again, a little more this time.

Then Spring, excited at the flushes and my one shot, suddenly stopped her prancing and froze to a point. There was nothing but a few wisps of grass and mud in front of her. Roy saw her from his side of the curving depression and stopped. "More mud?" he called. I didn't reply, and neither of us laughed.

The bird came up and flew straight out over the

open oxbow, in the clear. I dropped it cleanly, and it fell in front of Roy, almost at his feet. Spring was there as it hit the ground, muddy feet and all. She brought it all the way back, all the way across the mud, to me.

Before we had worked around to the end of the oxbow, we had put up two more birds. Spring pointed one, which I got, and Roy put one up wild. At the end we met, and we were back near the bank of the creek. But we still hadn't caught on, and we hunted up along the stream, and put up no birds. We hadn't gone far when we came to another oxbow.

This one was larger—longer, curving off to where we couldn't see the end of it, and wider. There was a twisting, stringy pool of black water in it. We did this one differently, both taking the same side.

Before we got to the end, Spring had pointed two woodcock, and one flushed wild. Roy took the first point and hit. We both shot on her second point, and Roy hit it just a little bit before I pulled the trigger. The wild one got away.

By that time, we had begun to penetrate the secret of the muddy oxbows. On the way back around the bigger one again, we put up two more. We got one.

"These misplaced shore birds," said Roy, as we rested on the bank, watching the currents roll around a log protruding into a pool, "are trying to get back to the shore."

"Apparently, it's the next best thing to an ocean

beach," I said.

"A muddy beach," Roy concluded.

We crossed the creek, after a bit, on a series of stones in a short riffle. On the way back downstream, we circumnavigated three more oxbows—two long curving ones (three birds around each) and one small, round pothole (two birds); we got only the latter two— Roy and I, one each—simultaneously.

Back at the bridge, we drew the birds at water's edge.

It took a while for this situation to sink in. Were the birds really attracted to these muddy edges for earthworms? Apparently so, for we found many probe holes and splashings on the mud. That late in the season, too, it must have been the kind of feeding habitat that would keep the birds later than other cover. True, the woodcock were not really standing right out on the bare mud flats—but they weren't far away.

We went back many times over the years. We never found the conditions exactly like that again, although we almost always had at least fair shooting, and frequently better. Some times we would spend most of a day there. Farther upstream—a mile—well into other tax-forfeit land, a small tributary of Alder Creek was dammed into an ancient, immense beaver pond, around the northern edge of which we never did get to.

But partway, at least, along alder edges, we also found more woodcock and a few spots which, for some reasons of particular habitat quality, always had a grouse in each.

But mainly, since this secret of ours was south of most of our coverts, and frequently on the way home, the School Trust Forty was the last stop of the day.

Besides, there was a delightful little grassy spur of sand on the *south* side of the road, out from a faded "No Trespassing" sign, that made the nicest place to sit and fondle a cold bottle and watch the sunset reflecting in Alder Creek's turgid surface.

CHAPTER 6

OF TROUT STREAMS AND TIMBERDOODLES

ALE green hues and earthy smells of creek bottoms in the spring flow imperceptibly into a hot, green, steamy summer. Finally, we detect the fragrance of aspens in a golden fall, and lucky are Roy and I in October, shotgun in hand, busting alder thickets alongside a same pool that produced fat, red-rimmed brook trout for us earlier. Luckier still, next spring with fly rod in hand, we remember the same alders in which Speck had tightened onto a woodcock.

In the fall, if the woodcock flight is not down yet, or too scattered because of a wet spell, Roy and I poke along riffles and search for trout redds, and maybe find a male brookie in his spawning colors. And if, in the heat of July, the trout are slow to rise, we abandon temporarily the rushing water for a quick survey of the year's production of young woodcock.

It is, of course, the bird's predilection for brushy creek bottoms and earthworms that brings it into the trout angler's domain.

It was toward the end of April one year, and the opening of the trout season.

April that year, even for Minnesota, had been a wet, cold one—a late spring, muddy high streams, lakes still ice-locked, and plenty of snow.

Roy and I did not go north to our favorite, the West Branch of the Mooselick River, but instead settled for more southern streams. We had hunted the southern coulees often, for both grouse and woodcock, and enjoyed the clear streams, misty hills, and limestone bluff country; but we had fished it very little.

When we got there—it was still raining—the streams we had planned to fish were up and swollen. Met not by the bright waters of fall, or the crisp sunny air we remembered from colored autumns, we encountered instead that dullness of spring when landscapes

are gray and cold, with not even the white purity of
snow. And lots of other people, attracted by the area's
newly acquired reputation for hatchery trout. So we
left in search of more hidden, smaller rills.

We found one on the map—Otter Creek—a tiny
stream that had eroded a narrow, deep valley not too
long. A two-rut trail wound up the coulee, forded the
creek a couple times, and ended in muddy tracks not
even we felt we could negotiate. The stream was
small all right, but tiny riffles alternated with some
fair pools, dropping over successive limestone ledges,
and it *was* clear, even in the light rain that continued
to fall, and there was no one else around. We pitched
our tent on a grassy flat inside a bend of the creek,
under a spreading white oak.

The fishing was nothing much—counting either
numbers of trout or pounds—but they were native
brook trout, brightly colored and fat. And we had only
each other to disturb the sounds of running water and
woodsy bird life, subdued by the soft mist that continued to fall all day long.

The trout we caught were just enough to smell
up a frying pan, though, and with enough other camp
fare, our stomachs were soon content. The rain
stopped, some patchy blue sky appeared overhead,
visible even after the sun had set, and promised a
bright day for the morrow.

We made a fire and settled down to the sounds of
crackling fire and creek riffles in shadows behind us.
Over our heads the sky turned to purple, still lighting

dimly a nearby opening of thin grass that probably had once been a farm clearing. High limestone cliffs seemed to loom higher in the dusk. There were no other sounds.

That is, until a demanding, miniature foghorn sounded from the nearby clearing.

Then we knew we were about to be witness to the woodcock's most private affairs.

The bass voice of the male woodcock in courtship is most usually described as a *peent,* and surveys of woodcock abundance are often based on peent counts. To me, however, the sound is better described as a very nasal *buzz* (but certainly a personal choice). And if you're close enough, you can also hear a little "hic-cup" from the bird, just before the peent.

After listening to several cycles, we could hear only the quiet of the stream, but we knew he had taken flight and was circling and spiraling upward, until he reached the zenith of his dance. We felt, rather than heard or saw, the flutter of dark wings in the purple sky. And then he returned to earth, plummeting back down, wing tips whistling in a liquid chirping that must be among the most melodious sounds of earth's avian life.

It stopped when he alighted to ground, almost at the exact spot from which he started, and then he repeated the whole routine. Over and over and over again.

Sometime after all of this, we presumed, the female slipped in quietly from the side, and the deed was done.

Stepping down to the Mooselick with heavy booted feet one early June day, from a steep slope onto a narrow bottom, a large, fat woodcock hurtled up from my feet. It didn't fly naturally, I thought. Instead it fluttered awkwardly through aspen branches that were still only slightly tinged with new leaves.

It wasn't quite a broken-wing act, but it was close enough to bring me to an immediate halt, for a horrible vision flashed of my hip boots already standing on woodcock chicks.

Not daring to move, I glanced down. Among the tan speckle of last fall's leaves, the random green of new growth, and a few brown patches of bare soil, I could see nothing. But I squatted, not moving my feet, and laid down my fly rod.

And then a small patch of painted earth suddenly moved and immediately scuttled away out of sight. And then another. They were so close to foot that I still didn't dare move. I looked for the two more I knew should be there, with no immediate results.

When a small companion happened by (Danny's

young friend, also with fly rod in hand), I called him over. His younger eyes, filled with fewer inhibitions and also closer to the ground, saw another chick not two inches from my boot, and finally the fourth. Fuzzy—and therefore out of focus—with incipient earth-probing bills an inch or so long, their buff markings identical to the tan of old alder leaves, the chicks were, to me, invisible.

With sufficient arm-waving on my part and small-boy rustlings on the part of Danny's pal, the two remaining chicks scuttled away into denser cover. Mama, presumably, was anxiously peering from some grassy clump a few yards away while we had inspected her charges.

I don't remember whether the Mooselick produced any trout for me that day or not.

The next day we tried to find the little family again, but with no success. Apparently Mama had had enough of fly rod-wielding, booted intruders and evacuated to remoter grounds.

Breeding in their northern summer range, most woodcock spend the snow-free days of the year in the northern tier of states from Minnesota eastward and the southern Canadian provinces from western Ontario to the Maritimes. The preferred habitat is young forest in early successional stages. In our northern country, this means primarily young alder, sapling-sized aspen and birch, hazel and dogwood, perhaps a young spruce or white pine—intermixed with openings.

But the requirement of a young forest presents somewhat of a dilemma to the woodcock. Young trees grow older and up, of course, and the required openings fill in, and soon a choice covert is no longer good woodcock habitat. Succession may seem to take place slowly to the fast eye of a woodcock hunter, but only fifteen years, or less, if left alone, is about the life of a good upland woodcock covert.

In prehistory, natural fires kept enough countryside in such a state of agitation that somewhere succession was always starting over. But the timberdoodle also finds its preferred habitat of young stages along creek bottoms—the so-called *riparian zones*— moist, low-lying strips frequently bordering streams.

The riparian zone is a unique, critical element of the stream-and-valley ecosystem—for aquatic life in the stream and many forms of terrestrial wildlife as well. For example, streamside brush provides vegetative detritus— leaves, primarily, and other plant parts such as buds and fruits—to the stream as food and nutrients to stream insects, in turn food for fish. A healthy riparian zone acts as a filter against damaging sediment and chemicals; it stabilizes streambanks, preventing erosion; riparian vegetation shades the stream, helping to maintain cool water. The riparian zone itself, naturally moist because of its proximity to water, is rich with its diversity of flowering plants, ferns, and mosses, and is often the habitat for many species of birds and mammals that could not prosper in the more arid, often cultivated, uplands. Not to mention woodcock and their earthworm foods.

Unfortunately, the riparian zone is also attractive to some of man's activities that tend to degrade its quality—livestock grazing, sand and gravel mining, logging roads, even our propensity to locate vacation homes on the stream edge.

So we can assume that the primeval riparian zone—without human activity—must have been quite satisfactory to evolving woodcock. Their summers, even now, are often filled with foraging and resting in moist stream bottoms.

In the fall, pushed by frost and northern storms, making inconspicuous flights by night, their solitary migrations southward to the warmer swamps and creek bottoms of the south Atlantic and Gulf states are little noticed. Here they partake of southern hospitality and southern earthworms for the winter.

Meanwhile, back in our northern alder thickets, the frost goes deep and earthworms deeper. But come April, streamside bottoms are the first to thaw, especially those with spring sources of water, and the woodcock are back even before all the snow is gone. In the openings, on spring evenings, there is courtship and woodcock singing and ancient rituals. Three weeks later, in the milder, warmer days of mid-May, four buff-and-brown fuzzy chicks in each nest hammer their way through egg shells and into a world of alders and earthworms.

During the summer, the juvenile woodcock's life is a daily routine of feeding during the night, mostly at dusk and dawn, and resting in cover during the day. At a month old, in June, the young woodcock can fly pretty well and is almost fully grown. During this time, it will eat its own weight in earthworms each day. Toward the end of summer, many woodcock can be seen, fleeting, ghost-like in the dusk of late twilight, by the traveler on lonely country roads.

But when the first cold, dry days of fall arrive, and he feels the old, instinctive twinges, the pace of life increases for the woodcock. Juvenile plumage has been molted for a sleek adult coat; he has been accumulating fat reserves for the long trip; and nocturnal flights become longer. And one night the southern hills beckon irresistibly, and a ragged wave of brown ghosts begins to drift down through the pastures and creek bottoms of eastern North America.

This is a time when the pace of life picks up also for woodcock dogs—and their masters.

A golden day in October, a good companion, the fragrance of autumn swamps and perhaps the nearby music of running water: All work their spell toward bringing out the best in dogs and hunting companions.

At least in mine.

One autumn day in late September, Roy and I moved across a wide, flat floodplain inside a creek bend, Speck casting back and forth in front of us. Up ahead was the muted rush of water through a small beaver dam. There were plenty of birds, and we had already had lots of action. Speck pointed at the edge of the water, a woodcock flushed, I dropped it far upstream, and it came down with a splash in the quiet water above the beaver dam.

Immediately, there was a roar of surprise and indignation from upstream. When we pushed through the bushes that grew at the edge of the beaver pond, we saw a fly-fisherman standing waist-deep, teeth solidly and angrily clenched on his pipe. He had, he informed us firmly, been working on a good rise in the pool, exactly where the woodcock had dropped—and put down the fish.

In a moment, though, he stopped grumbling, then chuckled, and admitted that he had hunted the same area yesterday—and noticed the trout rising in the pool. We ended up by his retrieving the bird for us, and all three of us settled down for lunch on the bank.

I admit I have a fascination, while searching out new woodcock hunting, toward the streams and creeks of an area. One of our favorite approaches is working the bottom floodplains of a small stream for a way, then finding a crossing on a fallen log or beaver dam or a boulder riffle, and hunting back on the other side.

There's a number of advantages to this approach. While Roy and I both always carry a compass, there is little need to use it; we follow the creek up, and then back down, and we're back where we started. Furthermore, the birds we miss often fly across the creek, and we have a second chance for them on the way back. Sort of double jeopardy, Roy says—for the woodcock, of course.

To anyone who loves the changing moods of natural environments and diversity of cover, the winding course of a small stream and the constantly inflecting music of running water at your side has no equal.

A more functional reason, however, is that in these riparian zones are frequently the very best woodcock coverts—and the most woodcock.

If you want to look up the woodcock in your field guide, don't look in the upland bird section. He's really a shore bird, ethnically speaking. But while the ancestral timberdoodle was indeed an habitue of shorelines and marsh, the press of evolution eventually pulled him away from his more aquatic relatives, and the woodcock abandoned his sea and lakeshore for the moist uplands and alder-lined creeks where, I like to imagine, he could listen to the music of trout stream riffles and smell the autumn popples.

Fortunately this lack of family loyalty landed him in the very places where trout anglers, if they could have their druthers for a place to hunt, would go hunting. That is, within earshot of running water.

Surely, the heavenly vice-president for woodcock evolution must have been a trout fisherman.

CHAPTER 7

YOUNG HUNTERS AND OLD PUPS

DAYLIGHT had not yet lightened the cabin windows. But heat from the wood range rapidly warmed the main room, while a kerosene lamp on my pine plank table flickered and filled the corner spaces with its yellow light. We were in our new family cabin, on a bluff overlooking the valley of the Blackrock River. Outside, an unusual morning wind scraped oak branches against the cabin's gable, and the odd acorn thumped on the roof.

Old Dave Kelsey, who had the eighty and an aging log shack across the bridge on the Blackrock, stuffed in another chunk of birch. The smell of coffee filled the room, and bacon sizzled in an iron skillet.

"It will be a wet day," offered Dave, scratching a two-day growth on his chin. I mumbled agreement, poking the bacon, and remembered that, so far, this year's October had been wet and cold.

But it was prime time, late in the month, foliage more than half gone, and no heavy frost yet. Already I had had several good days—with Roy or Danny, and my young Brittany, Speck, going on five now. And just day before yesterday, alone, Speck and I had had an especially fine hunt in McCullough's pasture on a late, hazy afternoon. Prime time for woodcock.

Our two Brittanies, Speck and Dave's male Ginger, alternately pacing and lying on the rug before the cold fireplace, occasionally eyed us attentively. Speck was reaching her prime, Ginger, an aging hunter, seasoned; they worked well together.

Up in the loft, still mostly in darkness, there were stirrings of creaking cot springs, thumping boots, and sleepy young voices—Danny, of course, and Dave's grandson, Chris. It was to have been a special day. A day when Dave and I were to introduce the two boys—both fourteen, neither one of whom had previously hunted with anyone else except their "dad"—to an "educational" hunt; to cooperation, to field ethics, to safety. We had planned it for a long time.

The four of us ate quietly at the plank table in the lamplight. While we were finishing, the wind gusted outdoors, and large raindrops pounded against still-black windows.

Speck and Ginger stirred slightly on their rugs. But, except for Speck opening one eye to check on my activity, neither looked as if anything was to be expected of them this day.

"Can we still go?" asked Chris.

"Yeah," echoed Danny.

Dave looked me straight in the eye as he stood up. "Sure," he answered the boys, but still looking at me, the slightest twitch of a grin at the corner of his lips. "Hay-ell, what's a little rain?"

"Good," answered back both boys in chorus, scraping the last bit of egg and doughnut crumbs from their paper plates. I groaned a little, inwardly, and walked to the front door.

Now the cabin faced east, and when I opened the door to take a first-hand look at the outdoor scene, the image was still as gloomy and wet as I expected. Both dogs scrambled out. The eastern sky was a charcoal gray, and only the waving bare limbs of the overhead oaks were visible against it. Even so, the coolness of the damp air felt good against my face.

"Going to be wet today, eh?" Danny said. But it was not a question; there was no disappointment in his voice. At fourteen, I decided, you didn't much care what the weather was like.

"Yep," I replied. "Hunting rubbers today."

When I turned back from the door, Dave was at the back window, peering out to the west, lighting up an after-breakfast cigar. I joined him. Through the darkness of the woods, up over the upper reaches of the Blackrock Valley, was a clear strip of plain, blue sky. The west wind was still blowing.

Dave looked at me a bit slyly, over his cigar, and said softly, "It's clearing." Not daring to hope too much, I mumbled agreement.

"Tell you what," Dave then announced, turning back toward the table, in a gruff and much louder voice. "Let's drive up to Thompson's and work over his back pasture. The creek bottoms there should be stiff with woodcock." (Big scrambling and sounds of approval from Danny and Chris; they didn't know a thing about Thompson's pasture, but Dave's words were exciting.)

I knew what he had in mind. It was close to six miles to Emmet Thompson's farm, where he mainly pastured beef cattle, a good twenty-minute ride by muddy township road. Then another twenty minutes over coffee in the Thompson kitchen (Emmet and his wife would insist), followed by a fifteen-minute walk along an open pasture lane toward the upper valley of Little Cat Creek. Plenty of time for the rain to blow away eastward and that patch of blue sky in the west to move in and get bigger. And it *was* good cover—the pastured fringes of the creek bottom with their scattered hazel and alder—that should be stiff with birds. I began to believe it myself.

"That sounds good," I replied. "Let's be off." (More scrambling from the boys.) Dave laughed conspiratorially and blew out the kerosene lamp.

Donned in rubber boots, foul-weather jackets, and blaze-orange waterproof hats, our arms full of cased shotguns, lunches, vests, and extra shell boxes, we left the dark warmth of the cabin and piled into the wagon, jammed in tight. In the back cargo space, Speck and Ginger, wet now and steaming, lay on separate pieces of old carpeting. Dave turned to the back, took the cigar out of his mouth briefly, and said, "My God, you two mutts smell just like *dogs!*" The boys whooped.

And I ground the old wagon into sound and action.

By the time we left the Thompson kitchen and headed down the pasture lane, the boys and dogs had reached the limit of their patience. The dogs were running and the boys were hopping. As we slogged through the muddied tracks of the lane, Dave briefly took his cigar, down now to a scruffy stub, out of his mouth and looked up overhead. I followed his gaze.

The eastern half of the sky was still filled with thick, gray cloud that occluded the morning sun. But the western half was the pure blue of a freshened morning sky, tinged with pink at the horizon edges.

And the rolling, turbulent edge of cloud was still moving rapidly eastward.

"A good day," Dave offered. "It will be dry by noon." I agreed audibly, but I knew it would be muddy underfoot this day. He had put his cigar back in place.

The lane rose slightly toward the north, but it was a gentle slope, and temporary. Up ahead the edge of the grassy pasture was sharp against the sky, and below, I knew, it dropped off into the valley of Little Cat Creek.

We got our first look at the valley when we topped the crest of the pasture rim. In the shadow of the retreating morning storm, it was a scene of soft color. Green pasture fell away from our feet toward the brushy bottoms and rose up again on the other side, a quarter-mile away. Hazelnut brush and scattered willow increased downward, until at the edge of the bottoms, splashed with the orange and red of blackberry leaves, the hazel and willow gave way to alder. From our vantage point, surveying the entire landscape, we could also see two patches of tamarack swamp; here the gold of turned tamarack needles contrasted with the dark green of black spruce. It crossed my mind: the edges of those swamps should hold grouse.

The four of us (or six, with the dogs) bunched up for a strategic conference. Dave took command. Jabbing with his cigar butt, he said, "Let's go straight down, cross the creek, and over to the other side.

Then we'll work the edge down-valley to the road,
cross again, and work back."

He paused for comment. It was a dry, colorless
instruction, including nothing of the action and
adventure that must be waiting for us down there in
the brush and cover along the little stream.

"Which way is down-valley?" Danny wanted to
know.

Dave signalled to the left. Three-quarters of a
mile, approximately, from this point west to the road,
the same north-south road we had left from the cabin.
Mid-morning now, we would be back sometime in mid-
afternoon. I was glad we had lunches packed and in
our vest pockets.

"Let's go," pleaded Chris. The two dogs, omni-
scient, were already halfway down.

I don't usually hunt with a party of four, usually
with only Roy. But in the last year or two, Danny had
been with us more often, to make three. Now, with
four, it was even more complex. By an unspoken
agreement, Dave and I would not be shooting much.
It was a day for Danny and Chris.

We hadn't long to wait.

At the bottom of the slope, we spread out in a
loose line and started directly ahead to cross the
creek. I was on the far left, then Danny, then Dave,
and finally Chris. The two dogs were ahead and in
front of me, in and out of sight as the cover thickened.

Abruptly, the hammer of grouse wings rose up
ahead, as the dogs must have put one up. The bird

came back out of the cover, low and fast, directly toward Danny. The grouse flared, then came my way. I waited only an instant, long enough to see the bird barreling at my head and Danny's raised gun behind it, before I dove for the ground.

Lying in the mud, it seemed one of those moments that would never end—waiting for the crash of a gun and the whistle and rattle of a load of number eights in the bushes where my head had been— waiting for the sound of a retreating grouse to fade away.

But there was no crash, no whistle of shot, no flutter of wings.

I jumped to my feet, eyes searching for Danny. His gun was down, his face intently watching mine. His expression was dead serious.

"Are you O.K.?" Danny shouted. "I didn't shoot."

I brushed off some leaf fragments. I laughed. "I'm well aware of the fact you didn't shoot." He grinned back. From the other side I vaguely heard Chris asking Dave what had happened and Dave answering something back. We resumed our march.

I supposed it was something of an insult, diving for the deck like that, implying that I didn't trust him not to shoot. With Dave or Roy I wouldn't have done that. But secretly I hoped Danny himself would do the same thing if the situation were reversed.

"Here's the creek," I heard from Dave. Presently we were all searching for a place to cross, and eventually we all ended up tip-toeing on the same log, without a casualty. Ginger hopped and splashed across eagerly; Speck, disliking water, took some persuading. On the other side, we were soon through the thicket of brush. And so far, no woodcock.

At the edge, I held back, and Dave positioned himself up on the slope with the two boys in the center between us. They were in the best of it. We swung to the left, to the west.

Suddenly sunlight flooded the valley. The edge of clouds had finally passed off to the east. Overhead was a brilliant, unclouded blue. And a slight breeze seemed to just come up, and it blew against our faces out of the west. *This is perfect,* I thought.

We hadn't long to wait.

Twenty steps, and both dogs came to a point, straight ahead of the two boys. Chris, to the right of Danny, stepped forward beside Ginger, and a woodcock rocketed up from the base of a small willow clump, quartered up the slope ahead. Dave held his fire, although the bird was in front of him, but at the crack of Chris's single twenty, the woodcock crumpled to the bare pasture slope. Chris and Danny both whooped, with Chris's "I got him!" coming through loud and clear. Both dogs bolted for the slope, but it was Ginger who picked up the bird and took it to Dave. Dave tossed it to Chris, saying, "You shot it— you carry it!" Chris grinned as he gently stroked the ruffled brown feathers back into place and then finally stuffed the bird into his vest game pocket.

"Come on, Speck!" Danny shouted from down in

the bottom brush, and both dogs came back down. Immediately Speck froze, near some large alders. Ginger saw her, stopped cautiously. Danny stepped up, and another woodcock bolted. It flew straight ahead.

From my vantage point, at Danny's left and just behind, I could follow every move of bird and shooter. This bird stayed down at the bottom, dodged first a large alder then a small clump of birch, then another alder. Danny's motions followed. Up ahead and towards the left was the thickness of a tamarack clump. But just before the bird would have disappeared into a wall of black spruce a tiny clearing opened up, no more than twenty feet across. With the bird in the middle of that, Danny's gun barked—and a small brown body fell to earth. A cloud of tiny feathers, side-lit by the late morning sun, drifted back toward us.

"Good shot!" I called. And it had been. I had not seen one better. Danny knelt to take the bird from Speck, gave her an extra pat on the head.

Up on the slope, Dave was—incredibly—relighting his cigar stub. His eyes caught mine, even at that distance, and they had a distinct twinkle.

"Let's go, dogs," I urged, and they did, rushing forward to work the edges ahead.

At one point ten minutes later we came onto a small open area in the brushy edge—hardly big enough to be called a clearing, fifteen or twenty yards in diameter, a low grassy mound. And right in the center of it Speck had frozen to a hard point. Ginger saw Speck and held back, not a very stylish honor, but sufficient. Speck's nose was only inches from the grassy ground. Danny walked up.

Beside Speck's immobile rump Danny stood. He took another step. Then another.

Nothing happened. Speck held solid, nose almost touching the ground.

Danny's jaw snapped slightly, repeatedly. I knew just how he felt. His gaze came down to the ground.

"There's nothing here!" he shouted. Speck moved not a muscle.

"There's got to be," I answered. "With a point like that. The dog knows it. Kick around a bit."

Danny did. And then Chris joined him.

"There's just nothing here!" Danny said again, now with a touch of disgust in his voice. "I can see—there's nothing here!" He was practically kicking Speck's nose.

"That's right," said Chris. "There's nothing here."

"The dog knows best," I said again. "Keep kicking." I walked over, thinking it might be a cripple, hidden under a tuft of grass. But also I remembered going through this same scenario once before, years ago.

"There's just nothing." Both boys turned toward me, their guns down at their sides, accusing looks in their eyes, as if to demand: *What kind of trick are you and your dog trying to pull on us, anyway?*

And of course the woodcock took that exact moment to burst from the vicinity of their feet and shuttle toward the creek and cover. Both boys literally ducked. And no one shot. Speck held, head up now, waiting for the shot and a signal to fetch. Neither came.

"I can't believe it!" Danny exclaimed, and he dropped to his knees to inspect the grass whence the bird had flushed.

"The dog knows best," I repeated, laughing. Both boys grinned a little sheepishly. And, shaking their heads and muttering at each other, they started out again. From my right, up on the slope, I heard Dave chuckle.

Behind the boys I paused briefly to sneak a look at the grassy mound.

I didn't believe it, either.

Up ahead, to my left, loomed another of the tamarack and black spruce swamps. I stepped through a tiny patch of yellowed marsh grass—and a grouse zippered his way out from under my feet, boring his way low and fast toward the tamaracks. A snap shot, and he tumbled at the base of a small spruce. Speck had leaped up at the shot just in time to see the grouse fall and was there in a flash. She loved grouse, and she soon had it in my hand.

For twenty minutes we picked our way along the edge. I was still in the thickest of the cover, near the creek. Danny and Chris almost shoulder to shoulder at the edge of the cover, Dave up on the slope.

Another grouse rose from Chris's feet and flew up the hillside directly at Dave. But Dave didn't dive for the ground. He stood fast and turned with the bird's flight, and when the grouse was fifty feet farther up the slope Dave's twelve-gauge roared, and the bird crashed into the bare hillside. Only then did Dave look back down to Chris, who still stood with his gun down.

"Nice shot, Gramp!" Chris shouted. Dave nodded his acknowledgment. And Ginger picked up the bird.

The brush thickened for me, and I had to move to my right to get around it. I fell in behind Danny for a minute, and then I stumbled my way farther and found myself behind both boys.

And then it was that the scene ahead unfolded to a picture that only rarely comes into an upland hunter's experience.

Both dogs, viewed from behind and between the two boys, were on a point. Both were on the same bird, apparently, one pointing from the left (Speck) and one from the right (Ginger); both dogs' noses, it seemed, almost touching. Between the dogs and me, the two boys had stopped.

Now, Chris was left-handed and held his gun at his left side. Danny held his on his right. Both looked alike from behind—same height and build, blaze orange caps, blaze orange vests, blue jeans. The spotting on the dogs was nearly the same—one left side, one right side.

The impression of looking at a typical hunting scene and its mirror image was so strong that I found myself for a brief instant trying to decide which was the real scene and which side was the mirror. But that brief moment was soon gone.

The woodcock flushed, two dogs leaned in different directions, two guns came up slightly differently, and two guns spoke—just as one woodcock, thrashing against the blue of the western sky, lighted to bronze by a noon sun, suddenly tumbled out of that sky, followed by a cloud of drifting feathers.

"I got him!" two young voices raised at once. And before the last syllable was out, Danny and Chris stood facing each other, suddenly still, with realization coming across their expressions until it changed to disappointment.

"Did you shoot?"

"Did *you* shoot?"

I know the feeling. First, the thrill of a good shot. Then, rapidly, the suspicion of another's shot at the same time. The question: Who hit it?

Ginger was coming back with the bird, but she deflected suddenly and trotted up slope to give it to Dave. He tossed it back to where the boys stood side by side. He didn't offer a word.

Danny caught the dead bird, and the two boys, side by side, examined it together, talking softly. Half expecting an argument, I stood and waited for them to reach a decision. It wasn't long.

The boys split apart, Danny still with bird in hand. Both were grinning. Danny took a step toward me.

"We," he announced, "just shot ourselves a woodcock!" and tossed the bird to me. I caught it, surprised, and the two boys immediately turned away from me, laughing, and started ahead along the edge, behind the dogs.

With a sigh of relief, I looked at the bird in my hand, then up at Dave on the slope. He was lighting his cigar stub again. And, again, his eyes twinkled as they caught mine. I stuffed the bird in my pocket and scrambled up ahead to take my place at the left of the boys, and chuckled too.

It must have been near mid-afternoon when we reached the road. We climbed up on the shoulder to the gravel, walked to the bridge over the little stream. It was high time for lunch.

Both dogs picked their way through boulders by the bridge to water for a drink, lay down in the dried grass at the edge of the shoulder. We emptied our guns, laid them aside, pulled out our birds to draw them at the water's edge.

It had been a productive morning. In addition to the two grouse that Dave and I had shot, we had put up two more; Danny and Chris had shot, but no hits. The boys had bagged three woodcock, and we had seen perhaps a dozen more. So far, two grouse and three timberdoodles.

We broke out packages of lunch. For the time being, all were content to sit, and rest, and eat. Below the bridge, black swamp water gurgled softly.

Danny, after a long period of silence, except for chewing noises, said between mouthfuls of bologna sandwich, "Any fish in this creek?"

"Not often," I answered. "It's dry half the time. Right now there's water in it because we've had a couple wet years, with lots of rain. When that happens, some minnows, probably, work their way up from the Blackrock. This is Little Cat Creek, by the way, that empties into the river in back of the cabin. Between here and there, there's a lot of good woodcock cover."

"And grouse?" Danny asked.

"Grouse, too."

He mulled that over, trying in his mind's eye, I supposed, to imagine the cover "between here and there." I thought back to many hunts along that part of the creek.

"What *are* minnows?" From Chris. I threw a glance at him, wondering if he were serious. He was.

"The word *minnow*," I started out, conscious of the need to stay out of a lecture mode, "is what most people call any small fish. But, technically, 'minnow' means a particular group of fish. Many of the minnows are small, like chubs and shiners. But not all. The carp, for example, is a minnow—"

"The carp is a *minnow?*"

"Yep—"

"Then what makes a minnow?"

I made a mental note to pursue the subject of fish with Chris later; I didn't mind proselytizing a bright kid into the profession of fisheries biology.

"Certain body characters," I said. "That is, certain sizes and shapes of body parts. Number and shape of their fins, number of scales, kinds of teeth, things like that. Technically, the minnows are called the—"

"Boy," Chris broke in with a grin, "I'd sure hate to have to count all the scales on a fish!"

"Yeah," Danny added. "I'd rather count all the woodcock between 'here and there'!" Old Dave, and both boys, whooped at that. I grinned, too.

The day was in full sunlight as we started back on the south side of the creek, only a low shadow in the east left over from the morning's storm. I began to wish I had my leathers on instead of rubber boots. We followed the edge of the bottoms eastward, back up the valley towards Thompson's and our wagon. I stayed down along the creek; Danny and Chris followed the margin of the swamp, ducking through willow and alder edges; Dave was slightly up.

We hadn't gone far when I bumped a woodcock from some thick alders. It flew to my right, toward Dave and the boys.

The bird veered in front of the boys, flying straight away, and Danny dropped it cleanly. Speck picked it up.

Then almost immediately Ginger locked onto a point, and Chris took it. It was a tough shot, behind thick brush, and the bird flew a long way before Chris finally got it off. Far ahead, down through a patch of medium-sized aspens, I saw the bird fall. We would really need the dogs for this one.

"I know where he is!" shouted Chris. "I think."

The dogs disappeared. Chris followed and, after a few minutes of walking, he stopped. In front of him was a small marsh, yellow grass blades thick and tangled. "It should be right in here," Chris said.

"A tough spot," I opined. Speck was barely in sight to my left over near the creek, Ginger was still out of sight far ahead. Chris began tromping about in the marsh grass, looking intently over the ground.

"Hold it," I cautioned Chris. "Let the dogs work it over." Chris stopped. I whistled.

Speck was soon at my feet. Ginger appeared, coming back. Neither seemed to have scented anything.

"Sometimes," I said to Chris, "a bird that's killed outright in the air will have its scent 'washed out' when it falls. Being dead, it doesn't give off any more scent. So the dogs have a tough time picking it up. Sometimes they can't find it at all."

Both dogs began to work over the marsh, but they gave no sign of scent. Chris stirred.

"I'm sure it's right in here," he said.

Danny, off to the right a bit, suddenly blurted out: "I see it—right over there." He was pointing about ten yards ahead, in the center of the small marsh.

"Show me where," I said, working forward and calling Speck.

Danny pointed it out again, and I finally saw the bird. Stone dead, partly hidden by the yellow grass. I stood by it, called Speck over to me. She walked right over the bird.

"Can't she smell it at all?" asked Chris.

"Apparently not," I answered. I reached down and picked up the woodcock. Then Speck saw it in my hand, jumped up.

I tossed the bird to Chris.

"You guys did real good—" I said to both Chris and Danny "—to spot that bird. I don't think the dogs would ever have found it."

Chris and Danny walked up ahead, shoulder to shoulder, talking. Chris was tossing the bird in his hand, softly and repeatedly, while they talked. Eventually he pocketed the bird, and they separated.

By the time we had hunted back, the sun, fiery orange now in its final flare of the day, was barely visible back through the brush of the creek valley. We had found one more grouse on the way (the boys shot and missed) and five more woodcock (Danny and Dave each got one). We were pleasantly satiated.

Turning to swing up the pasture slope, the boys lagged behind, chattering. Dave and I, quieter and perhaps more tired, walked ahead, our guns by our side, saying nothing. Up ahead, on the grassy slope, the low, horizontal sunlight drew sharp contrasts in the last of the hazel clumps as we climbed out of the creek bottoms. The late day held all the satisfaction of a good hunt now over—all the day's combatants were now to call a truce. No more sudden action; no more surprises.

That is, except one.

Both dogs, a little ahead and between Dave and me, were suddenly stock-still in the last little clump of hazelnut brush. Their white coats were flaming orange in the sun.

"Well, I'm damned!" Dave said, and I sensed rather than saw his gun come up. I took one step.

Up from the base of the hazel came the flush, up over the green-gold slope, into the darkening southern sky he flew, the setting sun reflecting bits of fire from his flashing wings. The ramming of my twenty double into my shoulder felt good. And with my shot, the little fires went out, and the darkened body thumped to the grass.

As soon as I fired, however, I had the distinct feeling that mine had not been the only shot. I looked over at Dave, whose gun was just coming down, and he was looking at me. We both knew.

"You got it!" Dave called.

"No, you hit it," I answered. "I was way under it—"

Chris came running up. "Hey, that was neat!" And Danny echoed, "Yeah!" behind Chris.

"Nope," Dave insisted. "He was hit just as I pulled the trigger."

"Nope," I said. "I could tell I was off—"

Now Speck came back with the bird in mouth, and Chris knelt. Unexpectedly, to me at least, she put the bird in Chris's hand. He stood up, and he and Danny put their heads together, examining the bird.

I took up the argument. "You got it, Dave," I stated quietly but firmly.

"No," Dave answered, "I didn't even—"

"All RIGHT! you guys," Chris piped, and, running over to me, popped the bird in my game pocket. "*We* just got our*selves* another woodcock!"

He hopped back to Danny. The two of them looked at me first, as if wondering how I was going to take it, then began to laugh uproariously.

I looked at Dave, feeling a bit sheepish, and suddenly he chuckled. Silhouetted now against the paling western sky, his face in shadow, he was pulling the wrapper off a fresh cigar. I began to chuckle, too, and then to laugh.

The boys ran ahead. The last sunlight was gone now from the grassy slope, and the hillside lay in shadow. With tired legs that plodded uphill, I still chuckled all the way.

And then I began to think of grouse and wood-cock broiling in the cabin fireplace.

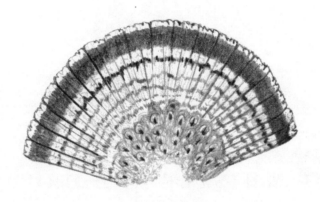

CHAPTER 8

THE WHISTLE AND DRUM

OR many years, Roy and I roamed over
the backwoods trails of Spruce County,
and some beyond, with my four-by-four
wagon. It bore the evidence of rocky
hills and hidden stumps and, in some internal
crevices, a few tiny brown feathers.

Our routes varied from tarmac country highways
to gravel byroads (usually passable) to remote logging
roads and pasture lanes. Some were so overgrown
with alder and dogwood that I'd have to lean back,

squint my eyes, and half-imagine an old set of tracks. A number of times, we hung up the wagon.

I'm not sure we got into better hunting in the remoter swamps and thickets, but when, after a tough ride in, we had good shooting—then of course we congratulated ourselves immensely, whether evening found us back home, around our regular campfire, or stuck somewhere in the bush.

In our part of Minnesota's north woods, old cutover lands were famous not only for grouse and timberdoodles, but white-tails as well, and Spruce County abounded with old "deer shacks." You couldn't call them cabins. The deer shacks were pretty much left empty, and kept unlocked, containing perhaps a rusty barrel stove and a crude table. Some had no road leading to them at all—squint your eyes or not. Most had a set or two of antlers nailed up somewhere on the side or front. A biffy out back, partly chewed by porcupines, usually constituted the improvements.

A few had names, though not many—most were not considered permanent enough for that—and these had only a rough board nailed up over the door with "The Past 50 Gang" or "The Apple Orchard" or maybe "International Diversified Holding Co." or just "Johnson." This last, in my opinion, lacked imagination. A few were not appropriate for reprinting.

One day along a pine-covered hillside that overlooked
a spreading marsh, actually an ephemeral tributary
to the Blackrock, Roy and I bumped along on a tilting,
rock-studded pair of ruts, and we spotted a shack that
right away appeared a little different than most. A
sign beside the doorway announced that it was the
"Quack and Snort"—obviously some old boys who
hunted ducks as well as bucks.

The marsh below the hill confirmed that.

Scatterguns in hand, Roy and I, with Speck,
picked our way around the edge of the marsh, and
where a sluggish outlet drained away through a floodplain of willow and alder, we got into good woodcock
numbers.

It was still early in the fall, and the duck hunting
proprietors of the shack had not, apparently, made
their first trip. The name, however, stuck with us.

Now Roy and I had a newly acquired eighty. It
was typical northern Midwest cutover—a mixture of
aspen and birch ridges and alder swamps, dogwood
and hazel, and some balsam spires stabbing up here
and there. Whoever cut pulpwood on it last (we
guessed about twenty years ago) left some old logging
tracks now grown over and—maybe because the log-
gers had had a nostalgic love for the great conifer
forests that once covered this region—a few towering
white and red pines.

There were three or four clearings of a sort, an
ancient cultivation of which was attested to by the
nearby presence of roughly mounded stone piles. In

one of these old clearings—a small one just about in
the center of the eighty, and upon which a grove of
high pines looked down from the clearing's edges—we
maintained our "campground."

An old logging trail led to it from the county
road, and my four-wheel wagon could usually make it
through. At first it was just a place where, each fall
on our first trip, we would chop down the bracken and
pitch our tent. Gradually, we made improvements: a
stone fire-ring; a board shelf for wash-up; a rough
biffy (soon chewed by porcupines); a table of aspen
logs and pine planks. We tried a hand-augered well
but hit too many stones.

A headwater of the Little Popple River ran
through alder and aspen saplings down below the
clearing, usually good for two or three woodcock flushes each morning during the migration.

One evening, early November, Roy and I stumbled up from the creek to the tent with two freshly
shot woodcock. A brittle sun was soon down behind
the creek-bank brush, leaving a pastel sky behind the
pines. We had a grouse from earlier in the day, and
the lot were to be our supper. We cleaned all three
out on our cold board back in the brush, with a dish-
pan of even colder creek water and, hands numb,
headed for the light of the tent and the beginnings of
a campfire.

I looked up at the pines sheltering the clearing,
and it was then I guess that I started to imagine there
a different scene: a warm, cozy shack—instead of a

cold tent.

We talked about it while the grouse and woodcock simmered in a skillet, and also later that night in our sleeping bags, some brush stubble sticking into Roy's backside and me tilting somewhat downhill on my side of the tent. We knew we'd have to thaw out the water jug before making coffee in the morning. And I guess it was then that we decided to really do it.

We remembered the "Quack and Snort," and the first time we came up the next spring, we were armed with chain saw, hammer and nails, some cast-off windows, a few concrete blocks, used plywood sheets, and odd and assorted lumber.

We were not interested in ducks and deer, of course, but rather woodcock and grouse. So when Roy pulled out a freshly painted board from his pack, he flashed a conspiratorial grin and proceeded to nail it up on the nearest pine trunk. It read: "Whistle and Drum."

It reminded me of when I was a kid and we decided to put on a circus and the first thing was to print up the tickets. In those years, faced with the real work, the circus planning never went any further.

The sign, I tried to convince Roy, needed an appropriate dedication. But convincing he didn't need.

Roy reached for the cooler.

The first job was to select the site and lay the corners with concrete blocks, accomplished rapidly and of course with much of the precision (we told ourselves) of a high-salaried surveyor laying out a major-league ball diamond. Decisions were no obstacle. We squared up the corners by making opposing diagonals equal in length, using a piece of string that had no more than six inches of stretch to it. The blocks were leveled with the use of a long piece of transparent plastic tubing, mostly filled with branch water from the headwaters of the Little Popple.

Next we laid the foundation timbers of used four-by-fours, notched at the corners and fastened with log nails. Next came two-by-six floor joists resting on the timbers, with ends toe-nailed in. Then these were covered with plywood sheets, and the floor was in place.

Outside dimensions so far were twelve by sixteen feet—roughly planned for a twelve-by-twelve building plus a four-foot porch in front.

By mid-afternoon we had all walls erected, of two-by-four studs and plates, with openings for a front door leading out on the porch, and a few windows—the location of which, again, presented no great decision-making. Local building codes and union standards, we concluded, were probably adequately conformed to. If not, we also concluded—while surveying our masterful handiwork so far, cold bottles in hand—the township inspectors probably would not be able to get in on our "road" anyway, even if they ever discovered us.

We knocked off for the day and, fly rods in the back of the wagon, headed for a lower reach of the Little Popple, ten miles away. And midnight found us squatting on the floor of our new shack with a half-dozen brook trout sizzling in a skillet on the Coleman stove.

We had a million stars for a ceiling, but it was our first night in the "Whistle and Drum."

The next job took longer. For three days we cut and shaved bare aspen logs of about four to five inches in diameter—eighteen for rafters, three longer ones for ridge pole and wall plates, two for inside ties, plus a couple extra poles to support the porch. It was a big job—interspersed with a little wood-splitting of ends and discards, a couple interludes for brook trout, and one trip out for more beer.

We installed the ridge pole with temporary boards fastened to the front and back walls, notched the rafters crudely with the chain saw, and installed them to the plate logs and ridge pole. After that we laid shiplap for a roof, covered that with tar paper, and that with an odd mixture of asphalt shingles that varied in color depending on what old lumber yard we scrounged cast-off piles of broken bundles from.

The result, we agreed, could not have been better

if we had planned it.

For outside wall paneling, we nailed up rough-cut aspen boards (sawed at a local mill from logs cut on our eighty the year before, with an idea for paneling Roy's den, an idea since rejected), laid vertically with narrow battens covering the cracks. We installed windows and the door, and left other details till later.

A week and two weekends of hard labor—a masterful job, we reminded each other, and congratulated ourselves again. The door we tied shut with a twist of wire against porcupines. That completed the job, for now, almost.

With gear packed into the wagon, and just before leaving, Roy attended to the final detail. He removed the "Whistle and Drum" from the pine trunk, and together, standing on the porch, we installed it very carefully beside the door. Backing away, and squinting slightly, it turned out not quite level, although still more or less parallel to the edge of the doorway. It was, we agreed solemnly, just right.

We slogged out our driveway in the now much lightened station wagon, our voices in perfect harmony on "Be it ever so humble," and our hearts light in anticipation of October.

On our first trip in the fall, we brought an old iron

stove—the kind with two cooking lids on top—
obtained in somewhat rusted but sound condition at a
local farm auction for two dollars. With some shiny
new stovepipe, we installed it approximately off-cen-
ter of the ridge pole, tarring around the cone fixture
through the roof. I suspect the local fire marshall
would have shuddered.

We had plans for further improvements—aspen-
pole bunks, a table, a counter-and-sink with a drain
pipe leading outside, some porch rails. But the woodcock flight was soon down, and, while we were working, Speck kept whining mournfully at the edge of the
Little Popple cover. So we soon abandoned hammer
and saw for shotguns and a dog whistle.

It was a good year, and the rusted old stove sizzled up a fair number of woodcock suppers, as well as
filling the shack at night with the warmth of blazing
birch chunks. We vowed to get back to work the following spring.

Next May, we did. At least as far as the installa-
tion of bunks, table, and a flat green chunk of oak
stump to serve as a step off the porch.

They were mostly days of bright blue sky and
busy warbler song. It was a time of burgeoning leaf
buds in the dogwood and alders, white splashes of
juneberry and wild plum throughout the woods,
bracken fiddle heads popping up in the openings. And
a few brook trout pan-fried on the old iron stove.

But one dark afternoon a warm, torrential rain
poured straight down for an hour, adding the essential

juice of life to the awakening earth around us. Standing dry on our porch, raindrops drumming on the roof and dripping through white pine needles high overhead, was purely delightful.

On our last day of the week, we worked in the woods—trimming our walking trails, adding a few rocks to a troublesome mud hole in our "driveway," dropping a large birch, and stacking up four-foot pieces.

We paused for a while beneath some old spruces along the south end of our eighty, a small crescent of a much larger marsh that lay spreading southward for a half mile. Most of it belonged to our neighbor, Elmer Olson. In its flush of springtime growth, it was an inland sea of tall, green grass across which the wind swept waves that swirled and heaved and (we could imagine) were sure to crash upon some distant shore. In the fall, the dry yellow stems and leaves would whistle and whisper noisily in northern gusts. Exactly in the center lay an island of jack pine and scattered small aspens and alders. And in that island cover—at certain times of the season, sometimes late, and only in some years—the explosion of timberdoodles rocketing upward seemed like a Fourth of July picnic.

At dusk, we trudged back toward the shack,

chain saw and shovel in hand, tired and happy. We passed along the edge of one of the clearings, where the trail bent around a rock pile, through aspen saplings that were slowly reclaiming the old field.

Far ahead, over the shack, dark masses of white pine tops bulged against the lemon-colored western sky. They were a welcome landmark.

But then our thoughts of lantern light and a hot supper were rudely interrupted: penetrating, nasal sounds emanated from the center of the opening—the *peent* of a male woodcock.

We stopped, and the back of my neck prickled with the thrill of this wild sound from the dusk of springtime. We were close enough to hear the bird's "hiccup" just before the "peent."

There followed the rush of whistling wings, spiralling up, up toward the zenith of approaching night, the flitting shadow of brown wings against a darkening sky, and then the tiny wingtip melody descending back to earth. Mrs. Woodcock must have been thrilled to pieces.

Before the peenting started up again, from in back of us near the edge of Elmer Olson's marsh, came a rolling tattoo that infused the darkening shadows on all sides. It rose slowly to a crescendo of rapid beating of strong wings, falling to a denouement of last faltering drumbeats. Back there somewhere in the darkness on a mossy log, Old Thunderer was calling in his lady love of the night.

We stood, silent then, transfixed. Old, familiar

sounds, these—born of ancient instincts that start life cycles anew and preserve the species. And presage the glories of an October to come.

We walked, Roy and I, still silent, occupied with our separate thoughts that were, probably, so similar. When the shack finally came into dim view up ahead, darkness was almost complete upon the clearing. We spoke idly of supper, a cold bottle, the hot stove.

But my thoughts were back on the trail, where the peenting sounded again, faintly audible.

It was one of those memorable nights when the "Whistle and Drum" seemed to be our most appropriate and welcome of human coverts.

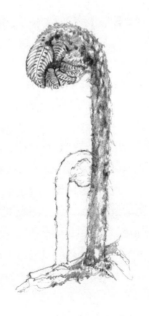

CHAPTER 9

EAST OF POPPLETOWN

IVE miles west of the "Whistle and Drum" was the greater metropolitan area of Popple, spread out in all its splendor. As I recall, it contained one filling station; an old building by the railroad tracks that still clung to a faded sign reading "Popple, Minnesota," although the Duluth Clipper no longer stopped; one saloon; a meticulously white church with a little steeple; and one large building so anonymous that no one knew what it once had been. Presumably, some residences were nearby but out of sight. We called it Poppletown.

The congeniality of the saloon's patrons, especially on a Saturday night, was legendary.

Our cover of interest was along the road between Popple and our eighty. Nothing really distinguished it. No creek, no pasture, no private owner. Actually, much of it was public land, a quarter-section outlier of the Redbank State Forest that mostly lay to the east of us. Roy and I developed no special sobriquet for it, and none ever seemed to naturally present itself. So never could we say, *"Well, let's try the _____ _____ cover this morning,"* or anything like that, and it was a bit frustrating. It was just *somewhere east of Poppletown.*

Next to the road lay a low meadow, stretching for nearly a half mile, thick with marsh grass and cattails. In back of the marsh was a distinct edge of thick woods, high aspens and mature red oaks. Not an attractive piece of ground, for woodcock. What lay west of the woods we were unaware—until a misty, cold day early one November.

It had been a late fall, with warm, dry weather stretching through most of October, and the woodcock flight had been late too. Northern birds had only trickled through. Those we found were fairly restricted to the edges of creeks and beaver ponds.

In the morning, we peeked gingerly out of a steamy window of the "Whistle and Drum" at dripping pine needles, thankful at last for the moisture of a

drizzly day, but hesitant about a hunt that promised
to be both wet and cold. It was mid-morning before
we cleaned up breakfast remains, put an apple in our
pockets, and donned foul weather gear.

We followed our "driveway" toward the county
road, and Speck was soon soaked through. But she
quickly pointed two birds beneath some aspen
saplings along the muddy ruts. Roy got one, the first,
and Speck leaped the driveway and brought it back.
Moments later the second flushed for me on the other
side of a clump of alders and I couldn't get it off. The
bird flew west, away from our property and across the
county road.

"Tough chance," Roy called. He stopped to fum-
ble out a red bandana from his inside pocket and wipe
accumulated drops from his glasses. I agreed, and
looked longingly in the bird's direction.

He might be down along McKennon's beaver
pond," I suggested, spitting away moisture dripping
from my mustache. Birds had been hard to come by.

"Let's give it a try," Roy agreed.

So we climbed up through thin oak woods away
from the drive, crossed the county road, and thrashed
through a bit of marsh grass to the edge of
McKennon's pond. Our neighbor across the road, Jim
McKennon, tried to assist the beavers a bit by tossing
in a few logs at the dam during dry years; he was a
deer hunter mostly and didn't mind us bird hunting.
Around the back side of the pond was an area of brush
and saplings which often held woodcock, and a hill-

side of mixed brush and larger trees sloped up from the pond where we had found grouse previously. Through the pond flowed the headwaters of the Little Popple.

On the far side of the pond, fog rolled irregularly up the slope, and the edges of the woods appeared only intermittently visible.

Leaving the marsh grass, we started into some scattered alder and, where it was a little drier, gray dogwood. "Whew, I'm wet," from Roy, and I agreed. And we were soon wetter as we plowed through the dripping dogwood branches. The mist kept up a cold pressure on our faces, but by now we had steamed up some from our exertions.

The dogwood looked like good woodcock cover, but we encountered no birds. Once Speck flash-pointed, but nothing developed. The one we had chased had disappeared. We continued around the pond's back side, and we had nearly come to the dam (on which we could cross, if we so wanted, in order to get back to our warm shack) when Speck locked suddenly into a hard point, facing away from the water. I looked uphill, through the mixture of mist and dripping brush, and took one step in that direction.

And our world suddenly exploded, like a string of Chinese firecrackers, with the thunder of many wings. Grouse—at least a half dozen. We had walked into a group, concentrated no doubt as they do in late season. Neither of us got off a shot as they disappeared up the hillside though the mist.

"Good Heavens!" thundered Roy. I glanced at him, standing wet and dripping, down nearer the pond's edge, and caught him grinning broadly. Silently I agreed, and spit more drops from my upper lip.

Speck was moving uncertainly, still smelling scent, edging toward the slope.

"We've just got to go after those!" from Roy. Silently I agreed again.

We made our way up the lightly wooded slope, came out on a bare ridge along which ran the thin line of a deer trail, plastered now with sodden oak leaves. We both stopped. And on the far edge of the ridge one of the grouse flew up wild. We crossed the ridge and loped down the other side. At the bottom was a small swale, grassy and brushy, and Speck got birdy. Two—three—more grouse, wild and lost in the mist ahead of us. No shots.

And on the siren called us. Out of the swale and up through more woods, down a slope to another pot-hole. Another flush of two birds at the edge, lost in the dripping cover. We followed, chasing our fleeting Pied Pipers up ahead.

Around the north edge of the pothole, in the path of the retreating grouse, we thrashed through brush and mist and wet grass, hunting blood up. Speck was, it seemed, continuously scenting birds. And we got farther and farther away from our warm shack, and closer and closer (though we didn't think about it) to Poppletown.

Finally we got a grouse. Or, Roy did—one that had stuck tight to the edge of a small swale until Roy stepped on it, and it made the mistake of streaking straight across the opening. It fell in the middle with a noisy crash into the stiff grass, gray feathers drifting briefly into the lighter gray of the mist that occluded the woods on the opposite side. Speck thrashed noisily and wetly through the marsh grass to retrieve it. But as she brought it to my hand, Roy took two steps away, and two more grouse flushed along the swale edge and disappeared ahead.

Towards Poppletown. Farther away from the "Whistle and Drum."

We passed through a lot of cover that could have held woodcock, but there were none. And each time Speck came on to a point of any kind, it was always grouse, farther ahead, flushing wild and hidden by dripping branches and fog.

And finally, we stopped altogether. Out of breath and soggy wet inside our foul weather gear, a cold mist against our cheeks, at the edge of yet another small marsh. Speck was at our feet, panting, resting. Or so we thought.

"I've run out of steam," Roy panted.

"I haven't," I replied. "I've got plenty inside this damned rubber jacket."

And then both of us looked at the dog at our feet and both tightened up at once. She was locked stiff as a log, nose near the ground.

Roy and I looked at each other across the pointing dog. Simultaneously we both found safeties with cold thumbs.

"Take it," Roy said. "I got the last one." And I took one step.

From under Speck's nose came a brown, fluttering form, big and noisy. Expecting the rocketing flush of a grouse, startled by disbelief, I stumbled over a downed limb and only got off a belated shot as the bird twisted through aspen saplings along the marsh's edge. As the woodcock wheeled around the far edge, Roy got off a long shot, but the bird kept flying and disappeared among the misted branches of high brush on the other side.

"I'm damned!" spit Roy. I spit some, too. I looked down and caught Speck looking up, her big golden eyes filled with reproach. Soaked as she was, she looked more like an orange and white mink that had just crawled out of the creek.

"Well, where the hell are we, anyway?" from Roy. I didn't really know, and I confided that to Roy. I only knew it was a long, wet, and cold way back to a warm shack. I knew as well that we were a lot closer to Poppletown than we had ever been before. On foot, that is.

"The Poppletown road will be easier walking back," Roy suggested.

"Full of mud," I said.

We checked our compasses, determined the direction in which lay the road coming east from Poppletown, and looked there, to the south.

Anyway, as it turned out when we looked again, that was where the woodcock had disappeared. So Roy took off along the small marsh's edge, Speck trotted ahead of him, and I followed both.

We were all headed, unknown at the moment, toward a rendezvous with our destiny of the day.

Through mist and fog, and dripping branches and sodden grass, Roy and I made our way around the small marsh, toward the south. At the end of the marsh, aspen saplings and oak closed in from both sides. We reached the area where the woodcock should have come down, but we never found it. Not there, where we expected it, anyway.

Instead, as we continued southward, the woods on both sides opened up, and in front of us now lay a broad, flat terrain of dogwood, hazel, and patches of alder—now widening on each side, east and west. Grassy clearings were scattered at random. The soil underfoot was moist.

We passed by the spot where the woodcock might have been, at first discouraged. Roy was to my right, Speck ahead. In a flurry of sparkling drops from the dogwood, a woodcock got up wild to my left, disappeared. And then ahead, Speck's bell stopped. The flushed bird?

"Point!" I called to Roy.

"Take it!" Roy called back. I did, expecting Speck to break point, as the bird had already gone.

But now two woodcock rose in front of her, one to my left and one to Roy's side. Two shots, and mine went down in the dogwood. It didn't take Speck long to find it, though through the mist and fog we didn't see it hit the ground.

From then on, Speck went from point to retrieve, retrieve to point. It was almost too easy, except for the uncertainty of limited visibility through the mist. Speck pointed into the fog; Roy stepped up; there followed a brown flutter and a muffled shot; a retrieve through wet dogwood branches. And then the same scenario over again, with me.

The flat area of dogwood was maybe five acres—wet underfoot, all branches dripping, the edges of the woods dimly seen on each side—and more woodcock than we could count. We didn't bother with wild flushes, rather only with the birds that Speck found and pointed, and often held back on those.

When the dogwood ended—abruptly at a colonnade of large oaks and aspens, and then another expanse of marsh grass—we stopped, out of breath. When we finished puffing, Speck was on point again.

I took the flush; the recoil still felt good as the bird exploded against the gray curtain ahead, and Speck bolted forward at my command for the retrieve.

We checked our compasses again, plowed south again through the marsh grass, and suddenly we were out of the marsh and up on a muddy road.

"I do believe this is the road east of Poppletown," said Roy, peering up and down the muddy ruts, and I agreed.

"Yes," I said. "We are—somewhere—east of

Poppletown."

It a was long trudge on the road now turned to a red, muddy slog of one and a half miles. I followed Roy, staring at his back through the rain. His orange game pocket gave for all the world a very nubile appearance, with the two little bumps that were his brace of woodcock.

Hungry as we slogged, the apples helped a little. But wet and cold, weighted down (some folks would question that) with our woodcock, we finally made it. Made it to a warm, dry "Whistle and Drum", a cold beer, dry clothes, and a sizzling supper of broiled woodcock with cranberry sauce, and butter-fried parsnips.

We hunted that cover many more times, usually in a dry fall. But the cover never dried out. It rarely failed us, and it never wore out. We never went to it that way again, though, but always from the Poppletown road. We got acquainted with Dick Allen, son of the owner on the east end of the Redbank forest land, and walked in on the Allen pasture lane.

It was hardly a secret covert. We just knew it as—well—somewhere east of Poppletown.

CHAPTER 10

DISTANT DRUMMER

E turned the wagon off the county road, bumped across the low ditch and into our driveway. The headlights picked up yellow flashes of wet aspen leaves on the ground, as well as those that flew from thrashing branches in front of the windshield. The wipers seemed to keep time with the gusts.

"A wild night," Roy offered.

Our "driveway," a twisting track of two muddy ruts, even muddier now with an all day's soaking rain, was usually impassable to all but a four-wheel drive vehicle, and tonight it was more so than usual. We ground through a low spot between alder clumps, up over a relatively dry hump between aspen saplings, and through scattered white birches that swung ghostlike in and out of our lights as we twisted and turned in the ruts.

The drive was close to a quarter mile, and nearly to the shack it dropped into a water-filled ditch emanating from a marshy pothole off to the side. The ditch, brimful now and flowing, was actually a headwater tributary of the Little Popple River, along which farther downstream we had had some fine woodcock shooting, as well as brook trout fishing.

But now the wagon lurched heavily and deeply into the ditch, and I had a moment of worry, but four wheels pulled us out, and we ground and mushed up through another pair of mud-filled ruts. The ruts ended at the end of our clearing, relatively dry and hard, almost surrounded by tall white and red pines. At the far end, crouched below one of the largest of the pines, was our "Whistle and Drum."

Tonight, with the sound of thrashing woods and smell of autumn in the wind, we envisioned the shack's bright and warm interior. It was soon to be a haven in a wild and swirling world.

Presently, we had our guns and gear unpacked, the lantern lit, the cast iron stove roaring with dry aspen and birch chunks, and a pot of coffee hissing on one of the stove's two lids.

We turned in early in the shack's two bunks, and as the silence and darkness returned with the lantern mantle's last little gasp of light, it seemed the sound of rain on the roof increased in intensity, drumming a steady tattoo that, for us, had always been the greatest of sedatives.

Sometime soon in the early part of the night, the rain and wind stopped, and I awoke, startled, perhaps, by the quiet. I could see through the cracks of the iron stove some lingering orange coals; warmth from it still filled the dark room, and I felt too warm. It hadn't really been cold outside, just wet, so I struggled with the sash of the old window beside my bunk and opened it a couple of inches. The fresh, moist air suddenly rushing in felt good, but I sank back into my warm blankets. I lay quiet, listening to the silence outside, broken only by the drip from tree branches and bushes, occasionally on the shack roof.

And then, punctuating that silence like the first explosions of a John Deere tractor starting up, came an unmistakable drum beat. Loud and obtrusive, now increasing in tempo, it rolled into a tattoo of machine-gun rapidity. The tattoo ended abruptly, but its impact lingered a while longer in the darkness outside the open window and in my leaping brain.

It was Old Thunderer, of course—off in the dark woods on a mossy log somewhere not too far away, beating away with wings that responded to an ancient programming. A few minutes later, I fell asleep as the John Deere started up again—probably with a silly smile on my face, but with no one to see in the darkness of the shack.

The morning broke clear and cool with an expansive blue sky brittle with autumn's clarity. But the woods were wet, and after breakfast Roy and I both donned rubber boots for the early morning hunt. It would dry off later in the day.

We walked back along the muddy tracks that we had so recently driven through—wondering how we had ever made it—toward a low area near the entrance of our driveway. It was a small patch of young aspens, through the middle of which our drive had been laid out, and it frequently held a woodcock or two. We walked in the drive; Speck worked both sides, from one to the other.

I said to Roy, "Did you hear the grouse last night?"

"The last thing I heard was the rain on the roof," he replied solemnly. "Until you hit the deck this morning."

Speck, who had found nothing to interest her up to this point, now began to act birdy. She was on Roy's side, approaching a small opening in the aspen saplings. Then, in mid-stride, her head dipped slightly, and she froze solid. Roy moved toward her back, I stayed behind him. And in an explosion of glistening water drops from the wet ground, the brown fluttering form of a woodcock rose and leveled off between the small tree trunks.

Roy's double barked once, and the brown flutter stopped in another explosion—of tiny feathers. Speck fetched.

"Nice shot," I said. Roy grinned appreciatively as he stroked the now thoroughly wet bird and then stuffed it in his vest. "Nice point," he said, jerking his jaw toward Speck, and grinned again.

On the other side of the township road the small stream that was the infant Little Popple had crossed the road and was dammed up by beavers. It was on the property of our neighbor Jim McKennon, good friend, but not there now. The beaver dam and lodge were old, and unkempt in some dry years, but now the pond was brimful, and there were many signs of recent beaver activity around the edge.

We turned to circle it, a walk of a good mile all around. The edges were usually good for woodcock, and sometimes a grouse or two. It was really the beginnings of the Poppletown cover. We decided the pond circuit would take us through the morning wet period, after which we'd head for the shack, coffee, and different boots.

The birds were there—we found about a dozen altogether, shot four, missed several, and flushed and missed one grouse. It was a satisfying hike that took us two hours to get back to the township road, and we were ready for coffee and, in the sunshine and warmth of mid-morning, some lighter clothes.

It was while we were walking across the road toward our own driveway that Roy said, "Could you tell the direction?"

"Of what?"

"The drumming grouse."

I chuckled. "Yes, I think I know where he was."

In the shack, we changed our boots and clothes, and made our coffee. I packed and lit a pipe, both of us sitting at our crude table.

"Up along the north edge of the Little Popple pothole," I said. "In that patch of black spruces—there's a log or two of old pine on the ground. That's probably the place."

"A good spot," Roy agreed. "I think I know the log, a mossy one. It's lying in on the *Sphagnum*."

"We can walk back on the drive to the ditch, and then cut up along the north edge of the pothole, through the alders and spruce. We should have him before lunch."

Speck beat us to the door.

The sky was still clear, but a little wind had picked up from the south. Warmer, a bit more humid, not as crisp as the early morning. "Maybe some weather moving back," I offered, as we trudged along the muddy track. Roy was quiet.

Reaching the ditch, we stopped. Looking to our right, up across the edge of the marshy pothole, now filled with slightly waving yellow blades, we could see the patch of spruce. We had heard no drumming.

"He'll be there," Roy opined.

Silently I agreed, and we stepped over the trunk of a large aspen, long fallen. We spread out slightly; Speck began systematically working the alders at the marsh edge.

Still no drumming. "Not likely at this time of day," Roy offered. "But he should be around here."

A hundred feet farther on, the *Sphagnum*-spruce patch was closer. And then, in the alder only ten feet from the marsh edge, Speck slowed and finally stopped, her nose low to the ground.

"Woodcock," Roy said, and stepped forward beside the dog. The brown bomb came up not a foot from Speck's nose. It cleared the alder tops, and Roy shot through the branches, and missed. The woodcock circled out over the marsh, wide open, swung back. It was in the clear for me but long, and I switched to my left barrel. I got off a quick shot just before the bird came back into the cover of the woods. It crumpled, far ahead, right into the patch of spruce.

I held Speck back. And we—all three—went on ahead, slowly. But immediately another woodcock burst from our feet and rocketed off through the alders, deeper into the woods at our left. Neither of us shot.

With our thoughts on the potential of the grouse,

as well as the downed woodcock up ahead, we continued almost on tiptoe. Speck was trembling, anxious for the retrieve. I still held her back. Then we were in the middle of the spruce patch, the ground under our feet spongy with the moss. It was quiet, dark with the trees' shade, cool. We saw nothing, heard nothing. The woodcock should be on the ground right in front of us. Speck was shaking.

"O.K.," I said finally. "Fetch."

She bolted, but stopped almost immediately, moved forward slowly. The downed bird was right in front of her, and in another second she had it located, picked it up, and brought it to my feet. I knelt down to take it from her. Roy was on my right, gun under his elbow.

And then the world exploded. Not five feet to my left. The thunder of heavy wings and the crack of tiny alder branches, then the brush of black spruce needles, and then the grouse was gone.

My heart was pounding. I had had a good glimpse, that was all, no chance for a shot. But enough to see it was a big bird, with big black shoulder ruffs and solid black tail bar. An old male. The drummer, for sure. And I saw then what I hadn't seen before, involved as I was with the woodcock retrieve— a big pine log, half buried in the *Sphagnum*, moss-covered and damp, probably originally five feet in diameter. It was the one I had seen in my half-sleep, last night.

Roy was laughing by now. "That's the log I was

thinking of, too." I sighed.

"Well, we know now where he was."

"And," Roy said, conspiratorially, "where he'll be again."

We circled a bit, away from the marsh and the patch of spruce, went through some aspen and alders, but no more action. The day was getting warmer, and I was sweating. And I was hungry.

"Time for lunch," Roy finally said.

I pulled off my cap, wiped the sweat from my forehead. "I'll buy the beer."

We idled around the shack after lunch, drew and skinned our woodcock, laid them in the cooler. Roy split a little wood. The weather was changing faster now, the sky clouding up rapidly.

"Let's go up the far side of the pothole," Roy finally offered, "circle the clearings on the north forty and come back on the north side of the marsh. That should about take in the afternoon."

"And come back through the spruce patch—"

Roy was grinning. "To end the day up right." And I agreed.

Speck beat us to the door again.

Heading away from the shack, we went deeper away from the pothole. The sky had clouded completely now, low gray masses scudding up from the south.

It will rain again, I thought.

And I also thought of that big male grouse back on the mossy log. Why do they drum in the fall? we had often wondered. Perhaps the same light intensity, length of day, angle of the sun—as in the springtime? Perhaps to lay out his territory for the winter and the following spring?

Was he the one we'd heard last spring when we'd been up cutting some wood and clearing the larger trees from our woodcock spot? How many years had we heard that particular distant drummer?

How many hens had he seduced on that mossy log in the spruce patch? How many of the birds that had ended up in our skillet back in the shack, over the past few years, had this bird sired?

We edged down a slope, broke through some thick tangles of deadfalls to the alders along the south side of the marsh, headed east.

"Should be some woodcock along here," said Roy, and broke up my wandering thoughts. Speck's bell jingled up ahead and then, sure enough, stopped.

The jingle stopped many times that afternoon. Along the south side of the pothole, east and north to circle two large clearings that once had been farmed. Old piles of rock, once pulled from the stubborn fields, were overgrown at the field edges and were now hidden. We must have put up another dozen woodcock, collected two more, and then stopped shooting. But no grouse.

The afternoon had continued to darken. The

breeze from the south seemed to carry even more moisture, and it felt like rain. Warmer, too, and when we stopped to take the last bird from Speck, I was sweating again. We had gone almost around to the pothole; the trail back led straight along the north side—and through the black spruce patch.

We squatted on the ground, backs against tree trunks, to rest and cool off. Speck lay down.

"Going to rain," Roy finally said, and I agreed. It was as dark as an hour later, normally. The shelter of the shack, and a supper of broiled woodcock, seemed now near and desirable. We were quiet.

And then—

Slowly, as usual, the John Deere started up. Speck's head came up off the ground. "There he is!" Roy whispered.

The heavy beats, the rolling tattoo, the final, defiant last strokes. "He's on the same log," said Roy, and stood up.

"I believe you're right. Let's go."

The black spruce patch was perhaps a hundred yards ahead. We went slowly, and after about two minutes, we stopped, listening. We waited, and it came again, louder now, beating through the moisture-heavy air like a jackhammer. We shifted direction slightly, crept ahead.

Speck pointed once, a woodcock, and Roy sneaked up beside her to flush it. I held her back.

Another two-three minutes and we stopped again. And again the drumming tattoo, louder now, nearer now.

"We should see the log pretty soon," Roy said.

We took a few more steps, peering through the darkening day, made gloomier now by shadows of the black spruce all around us. "I think I see the log," I said, half in imagination. More steps. I put Speck to heel sharply. She was trembling, sniffing the air.

It was time for another drum, but the shadow ahead was silent. The bird must be alarmed by our approach.

The breeze gusted sharply, and I felt the first misty spray against my face. I quickly glanced to the sky; the clouds were darker, but broken a little, and whiter holes appeared here and there in the south-west.

And just as I turned my attention back to the shadows ahead, the sky broke enough to allow a quick flash of hazy sun to pass through the spruces, and I saw the great, mossy log—much nearer to me than I had expected—and atop it was the big, strutting, male ruffed grouse.

"There he is!" I whistled through my teeth. "Can you see him?"

"I can't," Roy whistled back. "There's a big spruce in front of me—go ahead."

I took another step, Speck at heel. The flash of light darkened and disappeared, but I had the log located. The clouds broke once more, and now bright sun passed through the spruces to illuminate the bird in a wavering flood of sudden light. He moved, head high, thoroughly alarmed now, resplendent in his ruffed shoulders and fanned tail in the broken light and shadow—lord of his log.

Was this regal apparition really the patriarch of our eighty acres?

I raised my double slightly, took another step.

And then a sudden leap from the log, the roar of wings. He went straight away, through the only real opening that existed in the spruce patch. I slammed the gun to my shoulder. Speck bolted.

The sky solidified again, no white holes. The wind quickened, and the mist turned to real rain and beat on my cheek and my cap. The dark shadows ahead under the spruces darkened even more. The pounding in my chest went down.

It would have been an easy shot.

It was one of our all-time great woodcock dinners, as Roy was fond of exclaiming. We fried breasts and legs on bacon strips laid on the old pancake griddle. Fried raw potato slices, a can of jellied cranberries, a half-bottle of burgundy. Especially with the old iron stove going, it was warm and steaming inside the "Whistle and Drum." So we left both windows and the door open, even though some rain came in.

Outside on our little porch, we listened to the rain in the black woods. Nothing is so delightful, I've always felt, as standing on a cabin porch watching it rain in the woods. I had a last pipe, Roy a last beer.

"A great day," he said, with an audible sigh. "And an all-time great woodcock dinner." I was much inclined to agree.

It had been a long day, too, and we were both physically and emotionally relaxed. Tired, that is. We turned in early. The shack still warm, we left the windows open a bit, including the one beside my bunk. The rain stopped about the time we turned out the lantern.

Again the drops of water on the shack roof, louder now in the darkness. And the cooler air from the window felt fresh on my face. I settled deeper into my blankets.

And then—again—through the darkness and the silence of the woods and the dripping branches—all the way from a familiar, old mossy log in a patch of black spruces—came a familiar beat: the first tentative strokes, the rolling tattoo.

Lord of his log—sire, perhaps, of scores more much like him. The John Deere had started up again.

I could hear Roy over in his corner, chuckling in the dark.

CHAPTER 11

WOODCOCK IN THE SNOW

NE of those crazy-weather years came along when the summer was hot, and dry, and only frequent immersions in a cool trout stream made it endurable at all. And then came early September, a time when gradual relief was expected, when cool nights and changing country foliage drained summer slowly away.

But instead our continental climate pulled its usual practical joke: four weeks, almost solid, of gray, drizzling, cool weather, punctuated only briefly by an occasional clear night when hard frosts turned northern woodlands into premature and startling brilliance.

Still, our vagaries of weather were not over, and the next surprise was one that was not hard to take, yet unbelievable from day to day: October, that golden piper of excited dogs and breathless men with shotguns, stayed clear and mild for almost the entire month.

The effect of all this, we thought, was just as alarming to the woodcock that year.

Roy and I mulled it over many times, over coffee and lunch in the wagon, and we came up with a number of theories that really do not need to be repeated here. But the fact was that that year gave us some of the finest—and some of the strangest—woodcock hunting in all of our tenure in the aspens and alder swamps of Minnesota.

Perhaps the early hard frosts brought down the northern birds earlier than usual. Perhaps the mild weather all throughout October brought the migration to a temporary halt, and they piled up, like a series of rear-enders on the freeway, just at our latitudes. It seems reasonable. But whatever the reasons, piled up they were, and that year's woodcock season was superb.

The weather had one more surprise for us, however.

Roy and I had decided early in the season to make our annual grouse camp on the West Branch of the Mooselick River, the earlier scene of an occasional trout foray. We really weren't thinking of woodcock so much as grouse, for the planned weekend was late in the month and we would expect the woodcock to be gone from northern coverts by then, especially this year.

Friday morning arrived bringing an abrupt halt to the month-long weather idyll. Low, thick clouds and drizzling rain covered the whole of mid-continent. No wind, just fine mist squeezing out of a solid blanket of gray cloud. We drove for six hours, arriving at our campsite just after noon, and the dull color of sky hadn't changed a bit.

The weather forecast had not been optimistic either; the only change predicted was a gradual shift from rain to snow. With the warmth of the unusual October sun on our backs still a fresh memory, we shrugged the forecast off.

The river, black as ink under the dark sky, gurgled past us under streamside alders. We stared at the edge of the water and went through a little ritual of reminding each other of certain out-sized trout (or trout that had become out-sized over the years) we had taken at this spot or another. We had both heard each other's tales many times.

We set up camp in the drizzle, made lunch with some hot soup, foraged for some firewood, and cut it and stashed it under the wagon to keep—hopefully— dry. We kept the coffee pot going and listened to the soft rain on the tent roof. Speck had run around a bit when we had first arrived and now was soaked. After whining in first my face and then Roy's, wondering why we weren't getting out the guns, she resigned herself to her rug on the tent floor and curled up.

One spot in the roof had started to drip.

"Well," Roy finally opined, finishing up the last of a third cup of coffee, "we didn't drive all the way up here to sit under a wet tent."

"If you insist," I said.

"I'm not insisting too much," getting up from his stool. Speck came awake, shook, stretched, and jingled her collar. We donned foul-weather gear and broke out shotguns.

In the area where we camped, the West Branch was a tumbling, rushing stream, cascading down through a deep valley with close hovering hills. But just below us, the county road crossed the river on a rickety bridge, and downstream from that the river wandered across a wide, flat floodplain. In this downstream area, the river meandered through deep pools, and it was there we had often gotten down to taking some bigger trout.

In this lower section, the floodplain spread out a good five hundred yards on each side of the main stream course. At its edges a jumble of hills rose up a hundred feet, covered with a scattering of white and jack pines. But the floodplain itself was largely scrub-

by aspen mixed with alder runs and blackberry openings. It was an area we had often thought might
sometime produce some good woodcock hunting, and
though at times we had actually taken one or two, we
never saw any concentrations.

We always had been primarily interested in
grouse along the West Branch. The bases of piny
hills, where gray dogwood and winter holly mixed
with alders and an occasional small white pine, made
up some very slick grouse cover.

We stood on the bridge, hunched up inside foul-
weather gear, my jacket already feeling as if it was
beginning to get wet inside.

"We can take the left side," I suggested, shiver-
ing, "go down to the big bluff, find a spot to cross, and
come back on the other side."

"If you say so." Roy shivered back.

Speck was prancing on the road, not seeming to
notice the fact that she was more soaked than before.
We stepped off the road, headed for the base of the hill
to our left, and shouldered our way into some brush
that sprayed water back at us and down my neck.

The cover was unusually quiet, our footfalls on
wet leaves muffled to virtual silence. We didn't say
much to each other. Roy picked along the hillside, up
just a little from the bottom; I stayed down. We drifted through the brush, good-looking cover, around the
pines and occasional little aspens, through dogwood
still hanging with its white fruit, favorite grouse food.

But the birds escaped us. That is, all but one

grouse. I walked past it, and Speck pointed it behind me. When I turned, it exploded out of one side of a deadfall while I was hopelessly entangled on the other side and roared up the hill through the pines.

Roy nailed it when it was high on the hillside, still going up and almost to the top. Speck clambered up for it.

It was a big, heavy male, gray phase. Roy tucked it under his foul-weather jacket, a little grin stealing through the rivulets of rain on his cheeks. "Supper," he said, wetly.

But that was all. No more grouse. A quarter mile of grouse cover that looked top-drawer, a half hour of picking through wet brush, investigating a clump of small pines, shouldering through down branches. We paused to chew the matter around a bit.

It seemed we had had this experience before, on rainy days. Where did the grouse hang out? On dry-windy days they were up in the hardwoods or the jack pines, feeding on acorns, wild and skittish. On wet, still days, we seldom found them. We could only imagine that most grouse were holed up in the crown of a thick white pine, keeping dry.

"I'm fooled," I admitted to Roy. I also admitted to myself that that was the opening remark of an old dialog by which Roy and I would convince each other we should quit.

. Besides, we were soaked. My tin pants were so heavy I could hardly lift a booted foot over the next fallen log.

The dialog didn't last long.

"I trust the beer's still cold." Roy.

"And the tent dry." Me.

Roy was quiet on that one.

"The dog looks pretty beat out," I offered. She was prancing about, excitedly.

Roy agreed about the dog. I called her, and she looked back over her shoulder, with what I discerned to be a disgusted leer on her face. Aside from the grouse she retrieved for Roy, she hadn't smelled a feather this afternoon.

We hadn't gone as far as we'd planned, and we knew we couldn't cross the river here in this deep, flat section. I looked out at the brushy floodplain toward the river, covered with aspen and alder, with thousands of tiny branches glistening with millions of drops of water, just about as high off the ground as the back of my neck.

"We can climb the hill and walk back on the old trail," I shouted to Roy. As an afterthought, "There should be some birds along the trail." I don't think I fooled him; the trail would be better walking—and dryer—than the bottoms. I started up the hill, through the pines.

Fifty feet of climbing, and Roy stopped to puff and asked, "Where's the dog?"

I stopped, too. Where indeed? I looked back down, listening for her bell. There was only silence, at least only the silence of a muffled drizzle on my rubberized head.

I stared out across the river bottoms toward the stream. Up here on the side of the hill, we could get a better view. It was not really solid cover, a few tiny openings here and there.

I licked a stream of water running off my upper lip, staring out across that aspen and alder floodplain. Roy and I had the same thought at the same time.

"My God, that looks like good cover."

Woodcock cover, that is. Of course.

Then I saw Speck, or rather just the white of her flank, through the brush. She had wandered out toward the river as we had started to climb the hill, and now was silent and stock still. A hundred feet away. A hundred feet downhill and through dripping brush—locked on a solid point.

"Looks good," offered Roy.

I considered. A seam on the back of my foul-weather hood had started to leak.

"Aw, hell." And I blew the whistle. Speck started, her bell tinkled. Stock still again. I always hated to pull her off a point. She started again, stopped again. But that did it.

Up through the wet brush came a fluttering brown form, drops of water flying as it rose through wet branches. At the top of the alders, a woodcock leveled off, veered once to the right, and flew out toward the river. We watched its entire flight and saw it settle back down on the other side.

Roy and I were quiet, staring. The scrubby

aspen and brush cover extended all the way to the
river, across the river to the pine hills on the other
side, and all the way downstream as far as we could
see. A fresh rivulet of rainwater coursed down my
neck from the leaking seam.

I blew the whistle again, and Speck turned
toward us. We continued to climb, not speaking. And
as we did, a swirl of wind climbed up the hill, too,
strangely unfamiliar after the quiet drizzle of the
afternoon. The wind was unfamiliar in another way,
too—for it had a snap of chill to it as it brushed my
wet neck, and I shivered.

I looked out across toward the river. A single
aspen leaf, now disturbed by the sudden breeze, fell
from its branch, and slanted quickly down to the
ground. I made a note of the leaf's direction.

The wind was out of the north.

We sliced up the grouse breast, made some *hors
d'oeuvres* out of it on the grill and then put on a couple
T-bones. All under a tarp, keeping the drizzle out.
And halfway through the steak the drizzle began to
take on a more solid, opaque consistency.

By the time we rolled into sleeping bags, snow
was slanting down out of the north, in large, wet
flakes. The ground was white.

About the middle of the night I awoke to see

some strange patches of light on the tent ceiling and went out to investigate. To my surprise, the sky was clear, with millions of stars out; a big, silver, full moon shone through the pine branches.

A few wisps of cloud were still moving across the sky, high and fast. The strange patches on the tent were due to irregular accumulations of snow—and to moonlight filtering through the thin spots. The pine branches were loaded and bending under the snow's weight.

There were a good four inches of the stuff on the ground. The moonlight had turned the surrounding woodland into a silver fairyland.

I knocked a bit of snow off the tent roof and turned back in.

Early-to-mid morning we were in the scrubby aspen flats on the lower river. The snow seemed to cover everything, but a few open patches of ground still showed—on the lee side of a thick trunk, under a deadfall, under some blackberry still holding a few orange leaves.

We had taken the trail back down through the pines, retracing our track of the previous evening. The woods were still white, in spite of a brilliant blue sky and yellow-gold sunlight on the snow. It was wet snow, and much of it had remained on the branches—

most of it, it seemed, neck high. I couldn't decide whether it really looked like woodcock cover or not.

So far, we had seen nothing coming through the pines nor down the hill to the bottoms. So far, Speck had sniffed no birds, grouse or woodcock or otherwise.

We decided to angle across the flats, downstream and toward the river, a track of perhaps a half mile that would bring us to the river where the piny hills closed in and where we could cross on some logs. Speck was already ahead of us, working—and quiet.

"Hold it," I said to Roy. "The dog must be on something."

"No," said Roy. "I see her, over this way."

When I finally spotted her, I agreed. She was moving, but there was no tinkle of bell.

"Lost her bell," I said, and called her in. But when she came up I saw a different problem. The wet snow had clogged the inside of the bell, and it couldn't ring. I cleaned it out, but as soon as she ranged out twenty feet, it was closed again. Furthermore, against the white of the snow and a few brown patches of wet ground, she was virtually invisible.

"We'll have to watch her more closely," Roy observed.

And watch her we did. The dog nosed under alder clumps and blackberry, penetrated deadfalls, and did everything right, including staying within good range. Everything, that is, except point a bird.

I began to lose interest, stumbling ahead in the wet snow, my second pair of tin pants beginning to soak up to my knees. I soon lost track of the dog.

I tripped over some fallen slash, stomped out of it, and just as a woodcock burst from my feet, took a load of snow down my neck. Outlined clearly against a white background, the bird looked as big as a rooster. I got off a shot just as it wheeled around a snow-draped aspen, and the top of the aspen disappeared in a white cloudburst. I watched the bird wheel up ahead, unhurt, and out of sight.

I was stomping off snow, trying to empty out my jacket collar, when Roy shouted:

"Hey, Speck's on a point!"

I couldn't find her at first, peering at the snow and the scrubby cover. Then I did. A point it was, rock hard, nose close to the ground. Right in front of Roy. He stepped in, and the bird rocketed up from the dog's nose.

Snow glistened in the sunlight as melting particles shook off the branches in the bird's flight. It curved around toward an open area in front of me. I waited.

Roy's gun barked and the woodcock crumpled nearby. Tiny feathers drifted back to me, coming to rest on the snow surface like ashes from a winter campfire.

"Nice shot," I called, grinning.

Roy grinned back. "Maybe they're here after all." Speck brought in the bird.

And "here" they were.

It was like mid-October all over again—the birds

piled up, Speck moving from point to retrieve, to point again. Like October, except for the difference the snow made. I had never experienced anything like it.

There was no burst of bird out of a snowbank like grouse, no muffled roar like grouse, not even the soft rush of wings like woodcock. But timberdoodles they were, with the flutter and whistle of brown wings.

I tried to see what kind of ground cover a flushing bird came from, but never really decided. A bird would come up, dodge the snow-covered branches, and wheel through the openings, and I imagined they always came up from a clear patch, for I never found tracks. I would recognize grouse tracks in the snow—woodcock tracks I had rarely seen, and never saw that day. But there was no denying the brown feathered forms with long bills that Speck kept bringing in.

Actually, shooting was more akin to hunting in early season with the foliage still on, for the snowy branches cut down visibility. We missed a lot, in between hits.

Some of the birds simply flew ahead and stayed on the floodplain flats, some struggled up toward the pine hills, as if they tried to escape the wet lowlands.

On one occasion, two got up at once, rocketed up the hill. Roy got one, I got the other, and both birds hit snow-covered pine boughs almost at once, the resulting flood of snow from the branches almost burying the birds. Speck found them both. It was a new experience.

By the time we reached the lower edges of the

flats, found a crossing log and got over the river, our vest pockets were bulging pleasantly. And a last one we got just on the other side.

We had a long way back, through pine hills that bordered the far side of the floodplain, but somehow it didn't seem too long. Somehow that little extra weight in the game pocket made the booted feet a little lighter, even in wet snow.

And we picked up two grouse on the way back through the pines.

That night, we grilled four woodcock for *hors d'oeuvres* and feasted on fried grouse for a main course. We didn't have to do it beneath a tarp, but we had to don heavier clothes, for the storm that had passed had left some clear, cold weather for the night.

Sunday morning found us down on the lower flats again. We figured to repeat the previous day on woodcock, and then spend a couple hours looking for grouse before breaking camp and heading home.

The snow was gone, off the branches and most of the ground, so we didn't have the loss of visibility like yesterday. The soft ground, however, was no longer wet. The frost the night before had made the wet aspen leaves crunchy as potato chips under foot.

To make a long story—or rather a long, cold trudge of a half-mile through the scrubby aspen and back again—somewhat shorter, we found no more woodcock. We went all the way down, unbelieving, crossed the river on the same log, and all the way back on the floodplain flats—lovely cover. But Speck never whiffed a bird.

We spent our couple of hours on grouse, flushed about a dozen up in the thick pine ridges and got not one.

And so we broke camp.

And, like the timberdoodles that had enthralled us in such a flurry of snow and brown-butterfly flushes and silently executed retrieves, we, too, at last headed south.

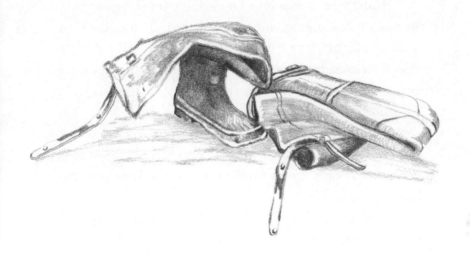

CHAPTER 12

WOODCOCK ACROSS THE RIVER

OY and I had a little trick.

Upstream on the Blackrock, maybe five miles from the family cabin, a little-used, two-rut track followed through the birch and red oak timber and then wound down the valley side, clinging precariously to the steep slope, to the bottom. The remains of an old bridge lay there in ruins, its center span long gone. The old road on the other side, whatever it had once been, was long grown over.

But there was a bit of a clearing on the near side where we could park and turn around. It was used as a campsite by deer hunters, later in the fall. And it was also used by many grouse hunters, for it was good cover along the river. We rarely found it unoccupied by at least one car or truck.

On both sides of the stream, the floodplain was flat and wide and bosky, with patches of alder and hazel, and some small birches scattered from river to bluff on both sides.

The near side was hunted rather heavily, we knew, mostly for grouse, but we knew of at least one other pair of woodcock hunters who used it often during the peak of the flight.

The other side of the river was good, too—and therein lay a problem. It was miles to the nearest bridge, either way, and no convenient fallen logs or stepping-stone riffles offered a way across. Even at the shallowest point (a quarter mile upstream), normal water level was knee-deep.

Across the river, the floodplain contained good cover, too. At a rapids, the river was only about thirty feet across. But with hunting shoes, or even rubber shoe boots, there still was just no way across.

We'd met many a grouse hunter looking fondly across the river, and we had looked fondly, too, and tried to look forlorn as well.

But, as I said, we had a trick.

It was an obvious one, and it shouldn't really have been difficult for anyone else to figure out. It was a simple matter of hiking upstream carrying hip boots, and when we arrived at the familiar shallow spot, we changed and waded over. On the other side, we changed footgear again, cached the hip boots, and were set for a half day in pursuit of timberdoodles, in good cover that we had all to ourselves.

On the far side, over against the base of the distant bluff, there was a run of alder bordering an old river channel that sometimes still had bits of water in it. Moreover, a number of small springs emitted from the base of the hillsides, and consequently, while other creek bottoms and upland pastures would freeze usually by late October, this run of perfect cover stayed wet and muddy for a week or two longer. It was the right spot for late in the season, or for an early autumn freeze-up. Late birds were always there.

Our method we kept a secret, chuckling each time at our skill and wisdom.

If, upon a rare occasion, we met another hunter along the trail on the near side, or at the parking area, we first tried to hide, or hide the hip boots, or quickly charge off into a thicket out of sight shouting, "I think he flew this way!"

Once we came face to face with another pair of hunters on the trail and couldn't avoid them. Curious about the hip boots we were carrying, somehow they seemed convinced when we earnestly explained that we were after fish bait. I think they were afraid to ask what kind of bait required shotguns, and they deliberately avoided us for the rest of the day. Our degree of secretiveness was equal to that we would exhibit if we were embarking for an amorous rendezvous.

As, indeed, we were—with a particularly lovely bit of woodcock cover.

On one certain day early in November, we tried to cross the Blackrock in this fashion, and the water was high.

Following some heavy late rain, the weather changed for the colder with the passage of the storm front, and the upland pastures had a good inch of frozen soil. So, naturally, we headed for the cover across the river. No woodcock were expected anywhere else.

As I said, the water was high. But we tried it, and the current, swifter than usual, boiled up near the top of our hip boots.

I had almost made it when I found myself balanced on top of a boulder about the size and shape of an ancient, slippery, 500-pound cannonball. I discovered, shockingly, that the water was about six inches deeper than my boot tops. Roy made it without sliding off the cannonball.

However—after emptying out my boots—we had a good day, and our bags were as heavy as a couple handfuls of woodcock could make them. In mid-morning the sun came out warm and bright. We headed back.

Speck had done a good job. And just approaching the water's edge, she made one more point under a clump of dogwood. *Grouse*, I thought at first.

But her head was down, and she was tight. And when the woodcock bolted, it rocketed directly across the river, straight-away, wide-open. I waited just long enough, and at the jolt of my twenty-gauge, the brown rocket tumbled to dry land on the other side. Although she hated water, Speck charged across.

Congratulating ourselves upon another clever and successful day, we changed into hip boots.

On the way back across, I stepped on the cannon-ball again.

And after that, I carried an extra sock.

The bluffs on the far side were broken in several places by dry ravines, and at the bottom of each there was always a small delta of flat land, maybe an acre or two in size, leading up a little valley. Coulees, we called them, after their counterparts in southern Minnesota. At some, the delta was littered with rocks that had been rolled down in earlier flash floods, but more often than not, the little triangular pieces were flat, moist with black soil, and scattered with young aspens and maybe an open, wetter area of horsetail.

Just why woodcock would select a patch of horse-tail, I don't know. But it often seemed there were more birds on these little deltas, and Roy and I would usually make a small circle in these spots in order to cover all the horsetail. When a bird flushed through the thick, hard, shiny stems, it sounded like a rattlesnake.

Maybe the soil was blacker and richer, washed down from higher woodlands, and fuller of earthworms. But our operation almost always worked.

It was also in the patches of aspen saplings that the odd grouse lurked and, occasionally, met his destiny in our campfire skillet.

And then there was the day of the boot-throwing. Roy had forgotten to bring his along.

Now, thirty feet did not seem too far a distance to throw a hip boot.

I waded over with my boots, got across to a dry bank on the other side, and changed to my leather hunting shoes. Selecting an open area on a small gravel bar, I wound up like a discus-thrower and let fly. The boot landed in a patch of dogwood almost at Roy's feet.

"Good shot!" he shouted, grinning. I felt like I had just downed a particularly difficult bird. Speck even tried to retrieve it. "Try the second barrel!" Roy shouted.

On the second boot, I had the distance all right again, but the deflection was off by about 30 degrees. The boot crash-landed in the rapids as if it were carrying a sudden load of number sixes.

Actually, it had almost made it, and, though submerged, it tumbled downstream, closer to Roy's side of the river.

Here, of course, was Speck's chance to make one of her historically most famous retrieves, but realizing she had been deceived by the first boot, she made no attempt to retrieve the second, unfortunately.

So Roy, hobbling on one sock foot, racing the current, with me shouting encouragement, caught up with the boot at a bend in the river a hundred feet downstream, and retrieved it himself.

The day was a fine one in late October, with sunshine and a light, crisp breeze. The alder runs and horsetail-covered deltas were rich with woodcock. And Speck had been in fine form. Our vest pockets were soon bulging with little brown birds.

On the way back, Roy went first, and threw perfect strikes with both boots back to me.

That part of it went well enough, even though I did step on the same cannonball again. A slow learner, Roy suggested. But we made it across.

It had been a fine day. We had our fill of woodcock, we even had two grouse, and we each had only one wet foot, about which Roy still grumbled a bit.

I loaned him my extra sock.

Magnanimously, I thought.

CHAPTER 13

CHARLIE AND THE JUDGE

UDSON P. Higgins was his correct name. He grew up in my hometown, a small town which was the county seat, rather inconspicuously. I say inconspicuously, because, although all the kids knew him, a little, and he played ball a little, and went to a football game once in a while, he was just never *conspicuous*.

He never got to be the pitcher in the ball games and never hit a home run, never got in any of the more significant fights in the schoolyard, never was

particularly noticeable in class, nor at the school par-
ties; there never were the tales of adolescent female
conquests told about him, usually told—truthfully or
otherwise—about the other guys.

The reason was because Judson P. Higgins was a
loner. And where he did some of his lone time, I found
out early one spring day, was along a little trout
stream, just outside town near my uncle's woods,
Middle Spit Creek.

Naturally, we called him Jud.

Pearl Harbor caught most of my gang in middle to
late high school, and upon graduation we all split for
one military branch or another. And with a couple of
tragic exceptions, we gathered back in the old familiar
Main Street haunts a few years later.

That is, except for Jud.

Someone said he shipped over, had got into Army
intelligence, and was in some sort of military legal
affairs in Europe. Sometime later, someone said he
was out but had then gone to law school. And then he
faded out of our consciousness. For many years, no
one saw him or heard anything from or about him—
except me, and I saw him just twice.

I was a bit of a loner myself, and I, too, enjoyed a
few hours along Middle Spit Creek. Both occasions
when I ran onto Jud were at exactly the same spot—

next to an alder-lined stretch of stream that held a deep, fast run beneath overhanging branches. One occasion was in the fresh greening of mid-May, and I came upon him just as he had hoisted a fat ten-inch brook trout from the water.

The second—along the same stretch—was in mid-October. I had heard a couple of shots and drifted over toward the creek, my own shotgun hung over my elbow.

I came around the alders and there was Jud, down on one knee, just taking a fat woodcock from a little black lab, whose tail was gyrating at a very high rpm. Jud looked up, grinned, and I grinned back.

"It's Charlie's first day out," he said, a little sheepish. "He's doing all right." I leaned my gun in the crotch of a sapling.

"Hello, Charlie." I took a few minutes to get acquainted with the pup, admired the bird, and since we were both ready to quit for the day, we walked back to the road together. Charlie bounced around through the Middle Spit alder thickets like a cottontail just jumped by a beagle.

It was many years after that that I got to know Jud again. In the meantime, Middle Spit Creek had undergone many changes—all bad—as the town gradually grew and spread out. Eventually the stream was channelized along the back of a supermarket parking lot, and even put underground for a short way. Needless to say, it was not in Middle Spit alder thickets that I saw him again.

Judge Higgins moved back to town eventually, bought the old Wickstrom place (former state senator, now deceased), and brought along a family. He was graying now but had the old grin, the old feeling yet of being a loner. The town took to him right off, and his family, too—brunette, jolly Myrtle, a litte overweight, two cute little girls—and a small black lab.

Yes, that's right. *Judge.* He'd lawyered about the state for fifteen years and now was back in the old hometown as a U.S. Circuit Judge, Fourth Congressional District. He looked like a judge, too—or a senator—and folks seemed to look up to him (even though he was a bit on the short side) and made it a point to jaw a bit on the bank corner or over coffee at Barnaby's on Main Street.

Pretty soon, it didn't matter whether they called him Jud or Judge, they both sounded the same. And eventually no one even bothered to remember his first name.

There were a few days, however, scattered here and there, when the Judge was noticeably absent from Main Street, or the courtroom, and the merchant or town father looking for some politicking over a congenial mid-morning cup could not find him. Mostly these days were either in May or October, and it was just by happenstance, on one of these days in the fall, when I was driving past his house, that I noticed the empty kennel at the side of his garage.

A little breeze had blown up a small pile of maple leaves along the north fence, but I could still tell that the little black lab was not home.

I brought two cold bottles from the refrigerator and set them down on the kitchen table.

"I wonder where he goes," Roy mused.

"There's plenty of places," I offered lamely. "Just because we've never seen him in our spots, doesn't mean he's not found some good ones of his own. I think he knows his woodcock cover."

"But how the hell do you hunt woodcock with a black lab? They're for ducks."

"I don't know," I said, taking a sip, remembering the day on Middle Spit Creek.

"I'd like to find out," Roy offered, hopefully.

"And how do you propose to do that?"

"Well—" another sip, a grin "—we could follow him out some morning, calculate about where he was heading, and then just—um—accidentally run onto his car parked somewhere—"

Now, spying on another woodcock hunter's favorite coverts, of course, is the nadir of bad field manners. We wouldn't be guilty of ever doing such a thing. Nevertheless—

Roy and I fretted about it all season. We didn't really spy on the Judge, although we drove a lot of extra miles around eastern Spruce County, just on the odd chance that we would run onto his car, the make, model, and license number of which we had committed to memory.

So far we'd not found him, although we did find some new coverts—and in one, way back in a really choice-looking pasture covered with hazel, we found a fresh spent sixteen-gauge shell, number nine shot. And on a nearby barbed-wire fence, a small bunch of black, straight hair.

"Pretty circumstantial evidence," Roy declared. But we toyed with the thought of how the Judge would treat such evidence in his courtroom.

One day after Carol had attended a gathering of the "girls" at the Higgins house, a shower of some kind, I had a brilliant thought. "Did you notice anything suspicious in their house?" I asked Carol.

"What do you mean, suspicious?" she asked, suspiciously.

"Well, shotguns, pictures of their dog on the wall, things like that—or, maybe, some county maps lying about?"

"No county maps," she scoffed, seeing through me immediately. "Besides, the place is always straightened up, not like some other places I know"—trying to catch a loose grouse feather on the kitchen counter—"I don't know how she does it, with those two girls around." Carol stomped out of the room.

She came back in. "Come to think of it, there was one funny thing."

"What's that?" I brightened.

"One time Myrtle reached in her refrigerator to get the dessert, and when she came out with it said something about the bait compartment being so awfully large. What do you you suppose she meant by that?" demanding an answer. Carol never let me keep bait in the refrigerator.

"Undoubtedly she has consideration for the Judge's cultural aspirations." Carol humphed out of the room. But she was presently back in once more.

"There was another thing." She sounded indignant.

"What's that?" Still hopeful.

"They have a faucet right by the kitchen sink. It has *beer* in it." Indignantly.

"Tap," I said quickly. "A tap to a keg, Carol. It's not a *faucet*."

"It's disgusting," she said and humphed out again.

I made a mental note to get better acquainted with the Judge.

The bait compartment was news all right, and I reported it to Roy first chance I had. News, OK, but it didn't help on the woodcock question.

We were down in southeastern Minnesota, in the coulee country, late in the season. Leaves were off now, and the big oaks that marched across the ridges of the looming hills were stark against a high, white sky.

"The Judge is the type I would expect to be a fly purist, anyway," Roy offered through a mouthful of bologna sandwich.

"I don't know," I mused, between gulps of hot tomato soup. "I remember on Middle Spit Creek—"

And then I *did* remember. Judson P. Higgins, in hoisting that brook trout out of the alder-lined pool, had a *Campbell soup can*, black dirt in it, on the ground by his feet!

Roy chuckled. "The old reprobate! We should ask him to come along up to the Mooselick!"

Now, Roy and I like to dry fly, most of the time, but we're not purists. The baritone slurp of a big brown trout in a fading evening light—or even the friendly plop of a little brookie—will make either of us reach for our fly box. But when the water's high and dirty and the prospects for a camp supper of trout are slim, we're not above shaking out the bait box.

"He'd probably clean it out," I offered. "I think he knows his techniques."

"He doesn't seem the type," Roy argued. "I think he would be very careful with his field manners."

"You're probably right," I agreed. I opened the wagon door, and Speck, who had been lying on a little windrow of dry leaves, stood up, tail-stump vibrating.

"Let's take him up next spring." Roy.

"We will," I agreed, reaching behind the seat for my gun. "Right now let's get up Himmelschmiffer's coulee."

"You're on."

I stopped short, wagon door still open. "I wonder how the hell he gets away with organizing a *bait compartment* in his wife's refrigerator."

Roy grinned. "He's probably got Myrtle convinced that modern refrigerators come that way!"

We headed for the coulee, the thought of modern refrigerators pleasant in my mind, following Speck toward the little spring creek that wound down from between the hills, gray and lavender now in late afternoon shadow.

It was early November, and there remained only one more weekend. Roy and I had been planning all fall to try out a piece of cover that was on the property of one of his co-workers at his shop. His friend was not a hunter, and he kept his piece of woods in northern Spruce County tightly posted. Still, he talked woodcock with Roy, and told him about seeing a lot of birds there.

Roy wouldn't ask, of course. But out of the blue, his friend had invited Roy to come in and try the woodcock hunting—and bring a friend. The cover had sounded good, especially for late season—a small valley, tucked away on a tributary of the Leaf River, a spreading spring seep with alders scattered through. We had had good luck with such spots before, late in the season.

We planned it for the Saturday morning.

But as luck would have it, Speck came down with a limp on Thursday, and on Friday it was worse. The vet couldn't find anything seriously wrong, allowed as how it was a muscle spasm triggered by a recent bump on the rear or a leg twist, and advised a week or two of rest.

That did it for her for the weekend. But Roy and I went anyway, alone without a dog, the first time in many years.

The day didn't cooperate, either—gray, windy, the kind of day when you couldn't be sure whether the cold haze you saw in the air was imagination or snow.

Roy had a key to the gate, and we must have driven a half mile to his friend's shack, parked, and took a compass reading to where the directions led. The little valley was a pretty piece of cover. The only color left in it was the bright green of watercress in the creek, around the spring seeps. But somehow the tang of it all was not there. We flushed two woodcock, got one, bounced out a half-dozen grouse, all wild in the wind and far ahead and never shot at them.

"Let's bug out of here and head for McCullough's," Roy suggested. "The back end of his eighty should have some grouse sitting tight in there today."

I agreed, but the day just didn't have it. And I just didn't want to put it into words: We really did miss the dog.

Back in the front seat, we dug out the county plat book, found a route back through unfamiliar country leading towards McCullough's woods, and to cover that was familiar. It was a rough road, though, and the wagon bounced us around. It was flat country, lightly wooded with aspen and brush. We cranked the wagon around a sharp corner, nipping the side of a massive, rotting white pine stump.

Roy peered ahead on the newly visible stretch of road, while I watched the ruts, some partially filled with water. He checked the map, then peered ahead again.

We both saw it at about the same time.

A little break in the brush on the right side, five hundred feet now: a car parked, partly out of view. Neither of us dared say anything.

And then closer, as we bumped ahead.

"I think—" Roy.

Closer.

"You think right!" I said, and jammed on the brakes. The wagon bounced once more, fifty feet from the parked car.

"It's him! We've found him!" Roy pounded the

dashboard with glee.

"Wait," I cautioned. "Check the license for sure—"

"I did already. It's him." Roy flipped up the door handle. "Let's check out the inside of the car, feathers, maps—"

"Hold it."

A figure had stepped out on the road, just beyond the car. A short figure, drab clothes, carrying a shotgun—with a little black dog at heel. He obviously didn't recognize our wagon yet.

I opened my door. "Better stay away from his car right now," I said in a low voice. "We're going to have to go out and face the Judge."

He recognized us as soon as we both landed on the road and Roy raised an arm in greeting. The Judge grinned.

"I'm afraid I'm caught," he said.

"Guilty," I agreed, with another grin, and the Judge came up toward us, breaking his gun, a well-worn sixteen double. The lab trotted up, too, expectantly, pink tongue jogging out with each trot.

Well, it turned out he had two birds. And he had missed a few, too.

"I've been expecting to run onto you boys out here sometime." I threw a meaningful look at Roy, hoping we hadn't written the Judge's license number down someplace in the wagon where it might be visible.

I knelt down to get acquainted with the little black lab. "It's unfamiliar territory to us," I offered. "We were just traveling between covers. How is it around here?"

Turned out the Judge thought it was a fine area. He had hunted here often, mostly for woodcock along a creek a quarter mile into the woods. Another tributary of the Leaf, I guessed. I stood up.

The birds were mostly gone now, the Judge opined, but still enough for a fair hunt on the last weekend. Then—

"Say, where's your Brittany?"

I explained about the limp.

"Too bad." The Judge was thoughtful for a moment. "Well—how about the two of you joining me and Charlie for the afternoon?"

"Well—" I did my best to be polite and not appear anxious to impose on his style of hunting. "Still Charlie, eh?"

The Judge grinned. "The fourth. He likes to play for a crowd—"

Roy and I finally consented, graciously, I think.

It was time for a bite of lunch, we all agreed. The Judge had thought it too cool a day to bring cold beer, he said, but he *had* worked himself pretty dry, and he seemed genuinely grateful when Roy opened the full cooler at the back of the wagon. We got on famously, and with Charlie, too.

I wondered silently just what it was we were supposed to do with Charlie in the woods—I was pretty sure that black labs didn't point.

"Charlie a pup?" I asked, tentatively.

The Judge smiled a little. "No-o-o. He's nearly

five. He's naturally small—got him from a friend in New Hampshire. Raises 'em that way, small—selective breeding, I mean—especially for woodcock."

I felt like my education was lacking. I wanted to ask, Does he point? Fortunately, I didn't. "How's he on ducks?" I opened a hot thermos.

The Judge smiled again. "No. I don't use him on ducks. Oh, he'd retrieve, all right. Or try, at least. But he's not big enough for a tough marsh, nor a big mallard. Your Brittany pretty steady on point?"

I gulped a little coffee. "Yes," I said, noncommitally. "Pretty steady." I was hoping Roy wasn't listening.

"I'd like to hunt behind her sometime," the Judge offered.

"Speaking of hunting—" Roy offered, draining the last drops from his cup.

"You're absolutely right," the Judge said. "We won't shoot any woodcock here in your wagon."

The country was pretty flat for a while, uninteresting, too much ground cover for woodcock. The day was darker, but still dry.

I expected, of course, to see the black lab coursing through the woods, hell-bent for chasing up the last woodcock in Spruce County over the far hills. At first, I didn't pay much attention to him, for he seemed to spend most of his time at heel by the Judge's feet.

But then, as we approached a dense oak blowdown, the Judge suddenly said, "Bird!" softly, and stopped. Roy and I stopped, too, but nothing seemed to be happening. Charlie nosed around the blow-down. I was puzzling over what it was that had clued in the Judge.

"How do you—"

I was interrupted by a roar of wings and the crackling of dry branches. A grouse bolted out of the blow-down, straightaway ahead of me. I shot, once—twice, and Old Thunderer dropped with a crash into oak leaves on the floor of the woods. It was a pleasant feeling.

"Good shot," the Judge said. I looked down. Charlie was standing still, hard at attention. I expected him to run.

"Fetch," said the Judge, still softly. And Charlie ran.

He brought the bird back to the Judge.

"That was nice, very nice." From Roy.

"First grouse all day," the Judge said. I had the distinct feeling that the Judge disdained grouse—some woodcock hunters do—and perhaps he disdained grouse hunters, too. I resolved not to shoot at the next grouse that got up, no matter where. Still—if he kept his worms in the refrigerator—

"Just over the hill ahead, now, is some fine wood-cock cover. The same stream I was telling you about, about a mile upstream. The area was pastured by a farmer on the next road over, till about two years ago. I wished he hadn't stopped—"

I mumbled a knowing agreement.

"—but he moved away. And trees are starting to

take over. Still, it'll be good for a few more years."

At the brink of the hill now. And it did look good. We three started down, leaving the woods. Charlie stayed at heel; I could never remember the Judge telling him to.

Near the bottom of the slope the cover thinned out. Small aspens were scattered, mixed with a few patches of blackberry and alders. It still had the look of being pastured. Another hundred feet ahead were thick willows where the stream bank dropped off to grassy edges and the water. The Judge turned to parallel the creek.

"We can work upstream a way," he said, "then cross on a beaver dam and come down the other side."

Roy and I nodded agreement. It was our technique, too.

Charlie was a flusher, of course, but he worked like he was on the end of a fly line. I swear he never got any farther away than thirty feet, except to retrieve a bird—and we had the chance to see plenty of that, too.

Charlie did, indeed, love a crowd. He worked for all of us, back and forth, pacing himself to our progress, glancing up only occasionally. The Judge made a very tiny whistle through his teeth, and each time he made it—which was not often—Charlie would turn.

Now he was in front of Roy, working slowly, tail spinning.

Softly—"Bird!"—from the Judge. And a brown

whirling form rocketed up, seemingly from nowhere, right in front of Roy, and he dropped it cleanly.

"Fetch!" from the Judge, softly. And Charlie fetched, bringing the bird to the Judge. He stayed at heel then, until the Judge gave him a quiet word. Immediately, he was working the ground ahead of us again, but never, it seemed, more than thirty feet away. We walked slowly.

The next time the Judge said, "Bird!" I tensed up. I began to believe in the Judge. And in Charlie.

Charlie was between me and the Judge. And two birds jumped, one each to right and left. I took the one on my side, dropped it into a clump of small birch. I had not heard the Judge shoot.

"Where's yours?" I asked him.

"He went out over the water," he replied. "I didn't shoot."

A thought crossed my mind. "Doesn't Charlie like water?"

The Judge grinned, accepting the nudge, but didn't take the bait. "He would probably find it in time. But maybe not. The willows are thick on the other side, and it might take too long." Chagrined, I agreed silently; I remembered a few times Roy and I had spent a good hour or so trying to retrieve downed birds across a stream, sometimes walking a long way around.

We drifted ahead. I kept wondering what it would be like to have Speck working over this cover, pointing, retrieving. I kept making comparisons with

Charlie. There's no doubt in my mind that the lab was effective. No doubt, either, that it must have taken a tremendous job of training to make him that way. Charlie simply did not run—he trotted slowly, if you can imagine it. He must have been sensitive to all the woods smells that dogs love, but when it was woodcock smell, somehow he let the Judge know it.

I asked the Judge again, "How do you know when he's birdy?"

The Judge grinned. "I really don't know how I know," he replied. "He just looks that way." I nodded silently; as good a way as any.

By the time we reached the beaver dam, we had three birds. Charlie had bumped up three others that we didn't get, and another one which had flown over the creek and we didn't shoot. "We'll maybe pick him up on the way back," the Judge had said.

And I guess we did, or ones just like that one anyway. For on the way back on the other side of the creek Charlie kept up his good work and sniffed out four more, two of which we downed.

I stopped comparing with Speck. It was simply a different kind of hunt. And I concluded there was no point in making comparisons; it was the diversity that counted. Absent, of course, was the heart-stopping anticipation in walking up behind a pointing dog. But instead was the thrill of watching a different kind of dog do his stuff, and doing it well. A good dog performance of any kind, I opined to myself, is nice to see.

By the time we had covered the far side of the

creek—a little different in that it was lower with more and thicker alders—the air seemed dryer. A little chill breeze drifted through the willows.

We crossed at a shallow riffle, balancing on rocks, while Charlie reverted to the instinct of his breed and took advantage of the situation to splash a little unnecessarily in the water. We climbed up the slope.

Partway up, we could see back across the valley. In the west the sky was clearing, a harsh yellow stripe lay across the horizon.

"Cold coming down," I offered, as we paused.

"Yes," agreed the Judge. And after another moment, "It's a pretty spot, this little valley."

"It is that," I agreed, watching the yellow stripe widen and brighten as the sun began to come down through it.

"You'll have to come with Charlie and me again to this spot. The new owner on the other side and I get along pretty well."

"We'd be mighty pleased to, Judge," I spoke for both Roy and me. Left unspoken, of course, was the accepted agreement that Roy and I would not come hunting in the Judge's favorite coverts until he did ask us again.

"Of course," I added, "if you want to hunt behind a real woodcock dog, a pointing dog—"

The Judge grinned. "I'd be mighty pleased to."

We started up the slope again, winding around the aspen and birch saplings.

Finally, the wagon came in sight, beside the Judge's car. Roy started for the cooler, and the Judge and I followed like kittens called to a plate of cream.

We raised the bottles to each other. Woods shadows were graying rapidly, but the last rays from the clearing western sky glinted off the brown glass. "Here's to Charlie," I offered. "To Charlie," was agreeable to all.

Roy smacked his lips after the first draught, cast a stealthy glance at me, winked just a little, then turned to our new companion.

"By the way, Judge," he said. "Did you ever fish the West Branch of the Mooselick?"

The next time I saw the Judge, he and Myrtle were in Damon's department store, back among large appliances. It was mid-April.

"Yes—yes," the Judge said. "I'd love to go. And the second week in May is good for me." He grinned. "I'll put it on the court calendar."

"The river should be just clearing nicely by then," I said.

"What patterns do you use that time of year?" the Judge asked.

I held back several impulses. Behind me Myrtle was in among refrigerators.

Dimly but clearly I could just hear her ask the

salesman about the bait compartment.

"The Hendricksons should be just starting to come off, Judge," I answered. "About number fourteen, I'd say."

CHAPTER 14

THE FARTINEST DOG

flurry of youthful arms and legs erupted in the back seat, fingers clawing for window handles.

"Methane alert! Methane alert!" And yelps of uproarious laughter from Danny and Chris.

I cast a look sideways at Roy. He was blinking his eyes, and then he, too, rolled down the window on his side of the front seat.

Chris tapped me on the shoulder from behind.

"Your dog," he informed me censoriously, "just *farted!*"

"I know, I know," I replied meekly, rolling down my own window.

"Your dog," Roy said, "has got to have the most powerful methane generator in the dog kingdom. The Great Brittany in the Sky would really be"—cough— "proud of her. We should figure out a way to put it into twenty-pound LP bottles"—cough, blinking of eyes—"and sell it!"

I looked in the rear-view mirror. The object of this excitement, Speck, stood innocently with head draped over the back of the back seat, wondering what the fuss was about.

With cool, fresh air rushing around inside the wagon, I drove on quietly and grimly, but kept my window down a bit, too. The boys were whispering in the back seat, then Chris grabbed my shoulder again.

"After all that, how can *your dog* ever smell a woodcock?"

How indeed? I'd often wondered about that.

Roy answered: "Dogs must have an AVC* in their nose—"

"Or in their brain," I offered, "that part of the brain that receives the olfactory message—"

"—they turn up the sensitivity when trailing a woodcock or grouse—and turn it down again when inside a car!"

---

*Kind reader: Roy, an old Navy radioman, was referring to *Automatic Volume Control* in radio receivers.

"Did someone say *brain?*" From the back seat, Chris. "In *your dog?*" Whoops and hollers.

I grumbled: "Passengers in the back seat had better watch their comments. Otherwise, they might be incarcerated in the dog kennel while the rest of us—ahem—gentlemen go hunting!"

There was a split second of silence in the back seat, and then: "Oh, no! Not in *that dog's* kennel!" More whoops and hollers.

The season was getting on. October would soon be gone, and the flurries that would announce the approach of winter could be expected any day. In fact, we had already had a wet, four-inch snowfall outside the "Whistle and Drum" that melted in two days, two weeks ago.

We had driven up the night before, the four of us and Speck, and bunked in for the night. We had started up in sunshine, but solid clouds had rolled down from the northwest, and by the time we ate supper, it was totally overcast, and colder. In the morning, however, a breakfast of pancakes, eggs, and country sausage had warmed spirits all around.

So we left the shack under a gray, fast-moving sky, heading for a day, perhaps, of old memories, a woodcock day that might be the last of the season. McCullough's woods first, then we'd work our way back north to a couple of coverts along Alder Creek. That was the plan. If there was still time, back at the shack, maybe a quick circuit around our next door neighbor's pasture.

Now, in John McCullough's driveway, Roy and I visited with him and his wife briefly. The boys stayed in the wagon. Our conversation went through the summer's drought, the lack of grouse, the prospects for the approaching deer season, and the McCulloughs' son's recent elk trip to Idaho. Mrs. McCullough didn't say much. I complimented her on the lushness of orange and yellow chrysanthemums that lined the front of the house.

Back at the wagon, the boys sat glumly in the back seat. All windows were wide open.

"She did it again," Chris said, matter-of-factly.

"Why didn't you guys get out of the car?"

"Well, we figured even she needed some sympathy after that one!" Both boys were grinning as they tumbled out.

We were soon suited up, booted up, gunned and shelled up, and we left the wagon and crossed the road.

Climbing up out of the ditch, we entered a grove of large birches—small, thumb-sized saplings when I first saw them many years ago—now ready for firewood. Many images flashed through my memory as we entered the old pasture. Here was a patch of hazel where Spring had pointed an unlucky pair of woodcock, the only double of my life; here a grassy swale (pretty much still the same) where a large, red-phased cock grouse had bolted in a rocket flight across to the other side and where, at my shot, it had crashed through brittle marsh grass to its final quieting—and where Spring had made a flourishing retrieve through the grass; a little farther on, here's where she made her last woodcock retrieve.

But today McCullough's woods were empty, almost. A half hour into the pasture brought us no woodcock. On a grassy knoll Speck made a nice point, held it for a brief moment, and then, fifty yards away, along the edge of a low-lying clump of alders, a grouse flushed up and quickly disappeared. None of us shot.

We walked our way deeper into the pasture, came upon the old swale, tributary to McCullough Creek, from which the beaver pond had disappeared a few years back. But no woodcock. Down by the old dam, we flushed another grouse. Speck had not pointed it; it had bolted out from under Roy's feet, surprised him, and both he and Danny had taken a fleeting shot, with no results.

"Why didn't the dog smell it?" Chris asked. But I didn't answer.

From the dam site, we trailed along an old pasture lane toward the road, single file. No one said much.

We drove north on the highway, then back east again. We crossed the Strawberry, Deer Creek, the West Jackpine, all streams that, at one time or another, Roy and I had hunted along. None of these had ever become a permanent part of our repertoire, but all held memories, sometimes of only one special woodcock under special circumstances. We were headed for a favored cover on Alder Creek, and maybe to some spring seeps along the Little Alder.

But heading south for a way on a dirt road, I suddenly pulled off. The landscape to our right had attracted me. Through a grove of maturing aspens and over a subtle slope lay the valley of the West Jackpine River. The small stream wound in lazy curves in the middle of its gentle valley, surrounded by birch and aspen saplings.

"Do you remember this one, Roy?"

"I do, indeed," Roy replied. "We went in there with both Spring and Speck once. Speck was a pup, and Spring was so old and lame we had to carry her back."

I remembered.

The property belonged to a man from the cities, of a very brief aquaintance, who owned much land in Spruce County and was himself a woodcock hunter. He had never posted his property.

"Let's give it a try."

We were soon down by the creek, four of us roughly abreast. Chris was on my left, Danny and Roy to my right. We worked the edge of the floodplain grass, then up the slope and out of a line of alders. A slight breeze drifted down the valley, and we worked into it, back and forth. Good cover, but no sign from Speck, who continued to work out ahead of us.

Then Chris, who had been hiking along in line on my left, suddenly left his position and came around in back of me. "What's up?" I asked.

"I forgot something," he said. He had a peevish tone in his voice and the twitch of a grin on his face. "I guess I must have been downwind from the dog!"

Then he laughed. I said, "Watch it, boy—and take your place in line!" But inwardly I chuckled.

Fifteen minutes later, Danny stood behind Speck in the middle of a little stand of small birches. She was frozen solid, her nose dipped toward the ground. "Go ahead," I said to him.

Danny stepped forward, and the brown bird rocketed up with wings thrashing through the birches. At the sound of the gun, the woodcock fell like a stone. Speck had seen it; at my command, she soon had it in her mouth.

Danny turned to me, his lips curving into a grin. "Nice shot," I said. It was, too. And I grinned back.

Danny pocketed the bird, and though we spent another half hour along the West Jackpine, in good cover, we found no more sign of birds. Well, after all, it was late in the season.

We left for Alder Creek.

The high point of the day—and most of our supper—was provided by some cover along Alder Creek.

Summer drought had left sloughs along Alder Creek almost dry, and muddy slopes lined most of them. We had tramped around some edges of these and then approached a larger, wider slough grown up with marsh grass. Chris was on my left again, Danny on my right, Roy farther over. And Speck was in front of Chris and me when she suddenly froze to a rigid point at the edge of the slough.

"Take it, Chris," I said. And he took two steps.

A grouse bolted then, rattled momentarily in the dry blades, and curved with increasing speed through alder and dogwood along the left side of the opening. Chris's gun flew to his shoulder. A tough shot, I thought to myself.

But when his gun barked, I saw feathers. And then the bird was lost to my sight.

"I got him!" Chris shouted. "He's down at that big dead tree! I saw him come down!"

"Fetch!" I said to Speck, and out she went.

It had been a long shot, a very difficult one, and now, nearly a hundred yards away, Speck nuzzled into brush at the base of a big dead elm.

She did not come up with the bird.

Circling, casting back and forth two or three times, Speck then left the big tree and trotted on, away from us. Chris looked up at me, disappointment flooding his face.

"I got it," he said. "I saw it come down. Why can't she find it?" Danny and Roy were quiet.

"Maybe it's a runner," I offered.

"But why can't she *smell* it?"

"Maybe she does," I answered. But I was not so sure. "Maybe she's following it." Speck was long out of sight.

"I know I got it!" Chris blurted out again. "It's got to be right there, right by the dead tree. That dumb, fartin' dog!" And then he ran, thrashing his way toward the tree.

"Hold it, Chris!" I called after him. "Let the dog work it out." But he stumbled on, crashing through the brush and dry grass. I knew how he felt; I remembered. Finally, he stopped by the dead elm.

For long minutes Chris stamped and kicked around the ground. Once I thought he picked a feather from an alder branch. Then, dejected, he stood looking in the direction that Speck had gone. Finally, he turned back, his gun hanging in one hand by his side.

And then, farther on, way out, bounding through the woods and brush, in and out of sight, came familiar flashes of white. Chris must have heard her, or sensed her. He stopped and turned, and as Speck finally trotted up to him, he went down on one knee. At that distance, I could just make out that she had the grouse in her mouth, as she came to present it to Chris's waiting hand.

I turned to Danny and Roy. "Speck found the bird! Chris hit it all right. It was a runner!"

And when I turned back, I could see Chris had Speck's head held tight against his cheek.

Farther upstream, we circled and meandered, but it wasn't until we arrived at the edge of a large, old beaver pond, lined thickly with brush, that we found our first real woodcock action. It was where we usually stopped and turned back. It was also where we usually found a few late woodcock, if any. And this time was one of the usual ones.

Alongside a small trickle that wound down from the main pond, in a narrow, steep-sided gully lined with spring seeps, Speck pointed four times. I think there was a total of six birds. And when the shooting was done, we had two timberdoodles in hand, one each by Danny and Roy.

Chris missed two shots, over two points by Speck. But each time he turned away with a grin on his face. *"That* was a good point!" he said, each time.

The overcast that had threatened all day closed in. At this time, end of the day, we were all quiet in the wagon on the way back to the shack. There was no light left for the neighbor's pasture.

Suddenly from the back seat: "Methane alert! Methane alert!"

Roy said, "Whew!" rolling down his window. "She's just got to have turned down her sensitivity on that one!"

A brief moment of silence in the back seat, all windows open. Then Danny said:

"I wish we had an AVC in *our* nose!"

A light drizzle was speckling the windshield before we got back to the shack. Soon the drizzle thickened. The speckled drops became small splashes of white. Images of a fire and a hot stove and broiling grouse and woodcock were welcome thoughts. It was dark when we stopped the wagon by the porch of the "Whistle and Drum."

Roy and the boys tramped inside, I followed. Speck disappeared into the darkness of bushes beside the driveway. I found the lanterns and some matches.

"You guys bring in an armload of firewood," Roy said to Danny and Chris. "Make sure it's dry." They trooped back outside.

I got two lanterns going. The boys came inside, arms full. Roy piled kindling and sticks in the old iron stove and lit it, and some wisps of smoke dribbled out into the room. Speck whined outside the door. "You guys let in the dog, will you?" I said to Danny and Chris. "Fill up her dish with dog food, too, will you? It's under the table."

"Just a minute," Roy said. He was still trying to build up a fire.

"Don't let her in just yet. I want to make sure I've got a *good draft going!*"

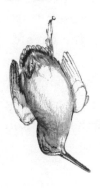

CHAPTER 15

A WONDERFUL DAY FOR WOODCOCK

EAT from the wood range hit my face as I came in the kitchen door of the cabin. I stomped traces of snow off my boots, a bit loudly, I suppose, and leaned my double in the back corner. Speck trotted noisily across the board floor, checked the cat's dish beside the stove, found it empty.

From the back bedroom, out of sight, came Ben's "Dad's home!" and then running feet. Carol was at the far end of the kitchen counter.

She said, "How was your day?"

"Great," I replied. "What's for supper, I'm starved—Yes, a wonderful day."

Ben had stopped in the middle of the kitchen floor. "Hi," he said, cautiously.

"Hi, yourself, Ben."

"How many woodcock did you shoot? Did you get your limit?"

"Well—" I hesitated. "No woodcock today, Ben. They're gone for the season now."

"None at all?" Carol asked, patently sympathetic.

"Nope. This cold spell sent them all south, I guess." I shrugged out of my coat. "Roy got one grouse. What's for supper?"

"Goulash. It's hot and in the oven."

I hung my coat up on the wall.

"Dad—" From Ben. Still standing in the middle of the room.

"Yes?"

"What do you mean, you had a wonderful day—if you didn't shoot any woodcock?"

The morning, in fact, had not been an auspicious one, not one to warm the heart of a woodcock hunter—nor anyone else, for that matter. The previous day had been one of falling temperatures and snow flurries, alternating with periods of brittle-gold sunshine and pale blue skies and southward-racing clouds. Not much snow stayed on the ground, though. The day before that, temperatures had been in the 50s, but a late October cold front had caused the mercury to plummet. I spent all day, Saturday, inside the warm cabin, fussing with some new cupboards. Two days before *that*, Roy and I had worked along the upper Blackrock in a literal burst of woodcock.

Carol and Ben and I had come up to the cabin for a late autumn weekend. Roy had agreed to come up on the Sunday morning.

And that morning—snow on the ground, air temperatures in the 20s, a low, gray overcast still streaking out of the north overhead—was not destined to be an all-time great woodcock day. If we'd been home, we'd have canceled. But there was no phone, and we *had* made our plans. I heard Roy's car crunch through the light snow outside the cabin, just as I was getting breakfast bacon into a big iron skillet.

I guess we're lazy. We always work the same old coverts, no matter the day or conditions. There's a satisfaction, I suppose, in being in the old and familiar—noting the growth of young woodlots and brush land, the water level of the creeks, changes in land use by the local landowner. Only when the old spots don't produce, usually, do we explore. And this turned out to be primarily a day of exploration.

We drove the wagon to the Blackrock again, parked it where we had been so recently. Our intention was not to cross the river into the alder thickets, but to another favorite area, farther upstream, where low, riparian willows stretched for a mile along the river. Three days ago, in the calm warmth of a golden late autumn day, the willows had been alive with woodcock, the air filled with whistling wings, brown bursts of tiny feathers, point after point by Speck, and handsome retrieves.

Today, there was no fluttering wings in the bare willows, now wind-whipped. Speck loyally searched out each opening among the branches, but she indicated nothing. "There's got to be one left," Roy hissed through stiff lips. "There just had to be a few who missed the last train south."

"We've never been clear to the end of this cover," I said.

"Let's hunt it out."

And we did. And at the end, where the willlow lowland ended with the encroachment of high, timbered hills, we concluded that the last woodcock had, indeed, caught the last train out.

Speck came up to sit beside us, tongue jogging out of one side of her mouth, her breath streaming into the breeze to be streaked quickly away.

"Let's hunt the hills back," Roy said. "Maybe there's some grouse."

It was an area we didn't know well. We turned away from the river, following a lowland which turned out to be a wide, tributary valley. The hills were still far away, but farther on and in the direction from which we had come, lightly wooded slopes came down to the low ground; the edge where slope met the willows ran parallel to the river's course and (we noted agreeably) back toward the wagon. We angled toward that edge.

When we slogged out of a swampy reach, the slope with its small aspens, scrubby oak and scattered spruce and balsams looked inviting. "Looks grousy," Roy said. I agreed, and perhaps 'cocky, too. But Speck found nothing. Roy followed a deer trail partway up the slope. I picked along the bottom.

The edge didn't last long, a hundred yards, but turned off, farther yet away from the river, and a smaller tributary valley opened up. It was flat, shallow, with gently sloping banks on each side, the dry channel of an intermittent creek winding through the middle. It was obviously pastured, and scattered throughout in just the right amounts were alders, aspen saplings, an occasional willow clump, some hazel. Under the bare branches now spread a light coating of snow, a half-inch thick.

We stopped, both staring.

"If there's one woodcock left," Roy stated, "he's got to be here. Just one."

"Let's try it."

And we tried, searched each willow clump, followed Speck through all the alders and aspens and young balsam. And not a sniff.

We stopped to puff a little. I surveyed the remaining upper parts of the little valley.

Roy chattered: "Where the hell are we, anyway?"

I dug out a township plat sheet from my pocket.

"This must be the back end of old Johannsen's. We're a half mile from his house."

Now, we had hunted a small bit of pasture on Johannsen's before. Not much, but we stopped there once in a while; there was a corner of his woods that almost always had a grouse in it and frequently we ended up a day there, just a half-hour or so, and collected a bird. The old man knew we were usually after woodcock, and he had invited us several times to hunt his back acreage, said there were many birds. But from his farmyard, it didn't look like much. We'd never taken him up on it.

We walked out of the little valley, followed the edge of the slope and back through the willows toward the wagon. A half-hour later we arrived at it. Roy opened his thermos—"good thing these things have such good insulation; kept the coffee from freezing"— and we followed with hot soup and cold sandwiches.

"That back pasture of Johannsen's has got to be top woodcock cover," Roy offered between munches.

"I marked it," I said. "It's a long way from the house, but he must have a lane we can walk back there on."

We agreed to try it early next season.

Before we completely finished lunch, a snow shower came up that literally blinded us. I turned on the wipers, but they couldn't cope with it. It seemed like a real blizzard. And then, just as suddenly, the snow stopped. The wind whistled a few more bars outside the window, and then it died down. I stepped out.

Overhead the sky lightened, the clouds had turned from gray to white, and in the north small patches of blue were clearly showing through. The clouds continued to move, and to thin out, as we watched. And in a few more minutes the sun broke through on a white, lacy woodland.

"Storm's over," I offered.

Roy climbed stiffly out of the warm wagon. "Do you think the woodcock will come back?"

I grinned. Just a little.

"Let's try upstream," I said. "If we make one big circle up along the river, over into the old beaver meadow and down back along the creek, that will about do the afternoon in."

"Not to mention doing me in, too."

"There's got to be a grouse there," I opined.

"I remember him from last year—as I recall, we left him in pretty good health." Roy shivered, looked around. What was left of the breeze shook down some patches of snow from a leafless branch. He whistled a little. "It's pretty."

So we made our circle. Through a snowy wonderland that numbed our feet and dropped snow packets down our neck and on one occasion slipped my feet from under me on a hillside and bruised my backside. And filled my barrels with snow; I took the shells out and blew out the snow, rubbing my hip.

Two hours later we were finishing up the circle,

slogging back along the little creek that emitted from
the old beaver meadow, birdless. Shotless. Not a
sniff. Both of us now wanted only to see the road and
wagon come into view. We weren't watching Speck, or
holding guns at ready, or listening for wings. Just
watching each cold, booted foot plod one more step
after the other.

We crossed the creek at our usual spot, on rocks,
started up the last little slope. And then—

"Hup, hup!" From Roy.

He was to my right forty feet, stopped. And
twenty feet to the right of him, Speck—white and
orange patches melding into the snow-mottled earth—
frozen solid.

Her head was turned to the right a little, lowered
just a little. Rock hard, pointing into a small downed
oak branch. She was right at the edge of the creek.

The hunting blood came up. Forgotten now were
cold feet and hands and tired shoulders.

Roy stepped up behind the dog.

The grouse bolted from beneath the branch,
thundered at first, and then came the sound of wings
strangely muffled by snow, on the other side of the
creek. I could see both Roy and the bird clearly. I followed Roy's bouncing gun and the bouncing bird in its
erratic flight. And when he shot, the bird tumbled in
a cloud of feathers and hit the ground in a rolling fall
and a shower of snow. It didn't move.

"Fetch!" I said. And Speck flew over the snow.
"Nice shot!" I beamed at Roy. It was, too—as clean

and difficult a wing shot I had ever seen.

Speck brought it back, a big cock-bird, heavy, mostly gray with a touch of russet brushed over its broad tail fan. She put it in Roy's hand.

When we reached the wagon a moment later, the low sun had brushed its own gold and russet over a snowy hillside. It was warm again, or so it seemed. I opened the cooler.

"Buy you a beer, Champ," I said to Roy.

A wonderful day? A woodcock day?

Well, it could be argued, I suppose. True, we had shot no woodcock, nor seen one. But we had been *hunting* woodcock—we'd found a new covert, to be tried next year.

Hunting has its detractors, of course. Those of intolerant persuasions, perceiving us as inflated masculine egos, are common enough. How do you explain to them that it was a wonderful day?

One could paint poetic pictures of the beauty of a tense dog on point, or the perfection of a difficult wing-shot, precisely executed by a favorite companion. But how, indeed, do you account for the happy forbearance of aching limbs and frosted eyelashes on a blustery day that blots the sun and whips spray in your face and snow down your neck? Or the delight of numb fingers on a hot thermos cup at trail's end?

And now I stand in the center of a room in my rustic cabin on the high banks of a favorite river, heat from a wood-burning range pulsing against my flushed, wind-frosted cheeks, and I search for phrases that will answer a ten-year-old boy's anxious questions. How, indeed, can I explain to him about a wonderful woodcock-hunting day, when I shot no woodcock?

Indeed, I cannot.

Not until the day when he himself steps into that magical scene behind a pointing dog in the alders, and feels the beat of thrashing wings. Not until he, too, tastes the sweet exaltation of a difficult shot, cleanly made; or senses the bittter ache of misses and empty coverts; or groans with the fatigue of a long cold day afield. Not till then will that agenda become clear.

And then, like the rest of us before, he should have the chance to answer that question for himself.

CHAPTER 16

THE HAUNTED ALDER THICKET

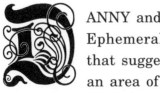ANNY and I found it, late one October. Ephemeral, indistinct, elusive—words that suggest but cannot define—it was an area of such superb woodcock cover that it might have existed only in our imagination.

Like a dream, we could find it one day, but it evaporated the next. We took compass bearings, established landmarks, broke down branches for a blazed trail—all fruitlessly. On perfectly clear days, with sunshine and shadows to guide us, and unobstructed visibility—it simply wasn't there.

But come a morning of swirling mists and invisible trails, and suddenly we would be in it.

Stark but familiar branches would appear like ghosts again—black alders against the pulsing fog, alive with the promise of wraith-like woodcock flushes and muffled shots. Too often we came away from those alders with a sense of awe and frustration, with the skin on the back of my neck crawling, only to take a compass reading back to the river and come out at some unexpected spot.

Haunted it was—not only by flushing brown ghosts, but with alder-thicket apparitions that appeared like miracles on only certain days, providing some of the finest woodcock shooting we ever had, but could never be conjured up.

Each year, on winter evenings, I dream of going back. But some years we go through the whole season without ever finding it, and the thought of it gnaws like a hunger.

Danny and I had taken to making at least a couple visits a year to some cover along the Blackrock, particularly in the lower rapids reach. Not that the woodcock cover was so good there, but the scenery was. It required some rough river-bluff climbing, and it was an adventurous change from creek bottom and pasture. There were usually some grouse there, and sometimes a few timberdoodles, too.

From our family place, we drove an old section-line road for a mile, then walked up an overgrown trail shaded with white pines to an old, rotting log cabin that overlooked a section of sweeping valley. It was a pretty place, and while the farmer a half mile back from the river always welcomed hunters to his scenic valley, he would never sell the little spot with the old cabin. It was just as well.

It was a long steep trail down to the river's edge, through red oak and sugar maple, young aspen and birch, and finally elms, red maples, and alder at the bottom. Our hunting track usually took the form of criss-crossing along the side of the bluff in pursuit of grouse, stopping now and then to catch our breath and view, from hillside vantage, the plunging cascades and black, shining boulders and yellow sandbars of the Blackrock River. The trail back up to the old cabin was always longer.

It wasn't possible every year, but after a dry summer, you could cross the river on the tops of rocks in the rapids, at least with no more than slightly wet feet. And on the other side were some small alder runs that paralleled the river in old stream chan-nels—always moist even in a dry year, always with woodcock.

When Danny was in his early shooting time, we worked those alder runs several seasons in a row, in a series of dry years. It wasn't easy shooting, by any measure, for it was thick, and I think it was here he developed some of his good shooting eye. The runs were always good for an hour's hunt and a bag of a couple birds.

I think other hunters rarely got to the other side, if at all. Downstream to the nearest bridge, below our cabin, was over a mile, including a broad thicket of high thornapple and alder; upstream were many miles; and in back stretched other miles of alternating swamp and woods. Deer hunters probably got to it, but their eyes were not for woodcock cover. Even at the end of a busy, mid-season weekend, we could finish up Sunday evening with a virgin covert.

Then along came a series of wet years. We couldn't cross the river, and we almost forgot about the little alder runs. We tried it once when we shouldn't have, and I slipped off a wet boulder and got wet up to my shell loops.

But a couple more years brought a drought, a bad one. Farmers complained of their parched fields, and agricultural economists gloomed. And I thought about the alder runs on the other side of the Blackrock.

Near the end of October, Danny was off work for a week before leaving for the navy, so we took a couple days in midweek to camp at the site of the old cabin, beneath the pines. On the way from our family place, we stopped at some favorite coverts, had good luck, and feasted that night around a campfire on broiled grouse and woodcock.

The next morning was a disappointment. We awoke, late, in the gray of a dark day, a fine rain spackling the tent. The drought, perhaps, was broken. Outside, fog lapped up the side of the Blackrock's bluffs and crept around the bases of the pines in the cabin clearing. We stared glumly at the shrouded valley with mouths full of scrambled egg and hot coffee. It was going to be a wet one.

Danny broke the silence. "Let's try the alder runs, anyway," he said. "If we're too wet by then, we can come back here for coffee."

I agreed.

We knew the river well, and after a wet slide downhill, we came out at the rapids, and crossed easily. Only Speck got her feet wet. By the time we clambered out of the streambed and started upstream toward the first of the old river channels, it had stopped raining. But fog continued to drift along the wooded bank of the river and through the brush. We couldn't see much, and it was the kind of day you wouldn't want to start out in new country.

The first of the little alder runs lay between the river and a low ridge, and a small creek came around the lower end of the ridge to empty into the river.

When we got there, all looked familiar—creek, ridge, and alders, even after several years. The fog lifted a little. We stepped over the creek, almost dry now, just where it came across from the end of the ridge, and out of the corner of my eye I saw Speck stiffening at the base of the ridge slope. She wasn't rock-hard, though, and I knew she didn't have one pinned down yet. But something was near. Then Danny stepped across the creek beside me—and a woodcock burst from underfoot and hurtled up into the fog. Neither of us had been quite ready for that one.

But Speck was still working on scent, twenty feet away. Another step toward her and then from our feet burst another woodcock flush, this bird following the first. We both got off a shot, both missed, and watched the bird disappear into the mist.

I looked at Danny, and he shook his head. "Poor shooting," he said.

"We weren't ready," I excused.

"No excuse," he replied.

Both birds had flown perpendicularly away from the river, not upstream through the alder run. Usually before, the birds we missed just flew up ahead in the old channel, not away from the river. And, strangely enough, I suppose, we had never hunted in this spot back from the river and the alder runs. We didn't know, really, what the cover was like on the other side of the ridge. But two woodcock were back there now, somewhere, and that made it seem like the best place to continue our hunt. The fog had lifted some more, and we could at least see well enough to make us think we knew where we were going.

We agreed on it, circled the end of the low ridge, found the creek again, and followed it up.

We stepped into a flat, misty valley, the little

creek bed deep but almost dry, in the middle of it. This was unfamiliar ground. And suddenly the fog came down again heavily. The sound of the river disappeared, and we were transported into another world.

"Spooky," Danny said. I checked my compass.

It was so quiet I could almost hear the compass needle spinning. Too quiet, really. For missing was the tinkle of Speck's bell.

"Where's the dog?" I asked, but Danny had noticed it too.

"I think she's over this way," he replied, and took a step to his left.

A brown ghost hurtled up, straight up, almost, over our heads, into the blinding whiteness of the sky. Danny's gun barked, and I could see just enough through the mist to sense the crumpled body fall, and disappear in the gloom ahead of us.

"Fetch," I ordered into the fog, and Speck appeared near Danny, only to disappear again. I whistled softly through my teeth to guide her back, and in a half-minute she laid the bird in my hand. I gave it to Danny. "Good shot," I said. And when I turned back to see what lay ahead, if I could, the fog had lifted again, and the flat valley spread out in front of us. Although the day promised to remain dark and perhaps rainy again, we could still navigate. And it still looked good.

It was a half-hour, I suppose, before we stopped to get our bearings again. We had shot another woodcock, after a brief chase, and it had taken us randomly away from the creek. The mist and fog had fallen and risen—never promising to clear—just some minutes darker than others.

I took a compass reading after first making a fuss about the direction back to the river. I was way off.

"Where's Speck?" Danny's question roused me from the spooky feeling brought on by my fussing with the compass. She was quiet, that was for sure. No bell.

"Up ahead—I think." We eased forward. But *forward* was only a term of expedience; there was no *forward,* or *back,* or other directions.

We had been working through many alders all morning, but now as we moved ahead there loomed through the mist a greater concentration of the scraggly bushes. First one clump, then another, and soon we were in the middle of alders all around. I drew in a sharp breath, stopped. So did Danny.

It was fantasy. It was, surely, a woodcock hunter's dream.

The alder area, in the middle of which we stood, gaping, was not too thick. There was good walking, excellent shooting room, but still the cover looked just right. We couldn't see beyond the second or third clump. The fog came down again slightly, lifted again. Although there was no perceptible breeze, shrouds of mist drifted slowly across the clumps to alternately soften and then reveal the starkness of the wild branches.

"Fantastic woodcock cover." Me.

"I don't know whether I like it or not." Danny. "And where's Speck?—I don't like it that she's gone and quiet."

I decided that we shouldn't stumble about looking for her—no doubt on point, and God knows where, in this fog—and blew the whistle for her.

Immediately there was the rustle of wings from a rising woodcock, off to my right, then the tinkle of Speck's bell, and a second later she trotted out of the fog. I patted her head. "Sorry, old girl." And then she was in front of us again, working between Danny and me.

For the next half-hour we had some of the greatest timberdoodle activity either of us were ever to witness. One by one, alder clumps came into view, ahead, right, ahead, left, then loomed up and passed on by.

The three of us—Speck, Danny, and I—went through the haunted alder thicket like a machine. A rock-hard point, a ghostly flush, a muffled shot, and a perfect retrieve. Speck worked faultlessly, never getting out of sight; our shooting was perfect; Speck's retrieves were the epitome of perfection.

And then, suddenly, we were out of it, at least the most of it, and Speck kept working without finding birds. It was as if we had stepped *out*—out of a magic land and into the world again.

I had no idea where the creek was, but we were

still obviously in the little valley. Still flat, still no landmarks, no looming hills.

"Let's turn around and go back through," Danny suggested.

I agreed. We did an about-face and retraced our steps back toward that magic alder thicket—or so we thought—and never found it.

It seemed the clumps should appear just up ahead, or over this way, or over that. But they didn't. We saw alder, yes—scattered bushes, some hazel, one large scraggly aspen that wasn't there before. We went ahead, to the right, to the left, wandered randomly, circled systematically. Speck worked hard, but came onto no points; Danny and I each flushed up a bird with our own stumbling feet but didn't shoot. Finally we stopped to face the bare, stark truth—we just couldn't find it again. Or—the back of my neck tingled—it wasn't really there.

Anymore, that is.

Danny shuffled his feet, peered into the gloom. "Spooky. Let's head for the river."

I fished for my compass.

When I looked at it, my guts said it was wrong—really *wrong*—though what sanity I had left said to still believe in it, and I had to grit my teeth to step out across that flatness in a direction I couldn't believe in, but in which the compass said we should go.

When we finally broke out of the brush to the river's bank, it was so strange to me that in a moment of panic I thought, *This isn't even the Blackrock!* I was in that frame of mind.

But a few minutes of casting about, and we recognized the spot—a good quarter-mile upstream from
our earlier crossing.

We thrashed our way downstream through
brush, found our rapids and crossed, and struggled up
the hill to camp and a pot of coffee.

It began to rain again.

We called it our hidden valley afterwards, for it
wasn't like being in a usual valley. It was really a flat
floodplain, with scattered clumps of alders and a
smattering of hazelnut, and small aspens here and
there. You couldn't see any sides to it. It seemed, particularly on a misty day, as if the flatness went on for-
ever. There were no outlines of ridge or slope on
either side, no distinctive trees, nothing particular
about any reach of the little creek—in short, no landmarks.

It seemed most seasons after that first hidden-
valley hunt the river has been too high. Danny was
gone for six years, and he had only one leave home
during the woodcock season. Fortunately that was a
dry year, and we tried the hidden valley on a
sparkling October day. We got some birds, but never
got into the alder thicket we looked for, at least so
that we recognized it.

Another dry year I tried it alone, again on a clear day, and didn't find it then either.

Once, on a misty morning, even though the river was high, I firmly decided to get to it—by walking up from the bridge below. The thornapple had me torn and perspiring and bleeding long before the time I thought I should be up to it. And then without warning I was there.

In the middle of it again. With all my puffing and sweating and swearing, I was suddenly cold all over, the back of my neck tingling again. The alder clumps, just as before, appeared and disappeared and reappeared in the fog. Speck drifted soundlessly to point after point, my little double couldn't miss, and one bird after another crumpled and fell through the fog. I compassed over to the river and struggled back along it to the bridge and my wagon, thinking I would never make it, vowing never to do it again that way.

Danny's out now, and he and I and Roy try to get over to the magic alder thicket whenever we can. Sometimes we find it, sometimes not.

In the hard objectivity of noon on a sunny day, I can talk myself into the solution. It is obviously (I say to myself, boldly) a matter of being able, on a clear day, to see everything for a great distance, and no particular area stands out. It's there, but you can't see it.

It's just that simple.

But in the flicker of an evening campfire over-looking the Blackrock Valley, knowing that that damned covert is across there, somewhere, and I can't find it when I want to, I say you can't be so objective about it. For, when I'm there in the gloom of a misty morning, never mind the cold, objective solution to what I've convinced myself is an optical illusion.

When my skin crawls and I *know* I've found it once again, then I'm immersed in the swirling fog and the looming alders, with a rock-hard pointing Brittany, with ghost-like flushes and crumpling birds and small brown feathers that drift away to become part of the substance of the fog itself—then the haunt-ed alder thicket engulfs my whole being. I have passed through a portal into a world of unreality that is part witchery—and part paradise.

CHAPTER 17

McCULLOUGH'S BEAVER POND

URING those early years that Roy and I hunted in John McCullough's pastured woodlot, we found most of our woodcock either scattered around the edges of the small swales or along the creek. And while the wood-lot had been one of my very earliest and choicest coverts, it changed in later years, particularly when John McCullough stopped pasturing it. Oak trees replaced dogwood and other brush, and openings closed in. Even though John's son later also ran cattle in it, the woodlot as a whole never approached the halcyon days of the early years.

One of the older, favored parts of the woodlot was a long, low grassy run with sloping, brushy sides that ran diagonally almost through the entire eighty. It was not a swale as such, but rather actually a dry tributary of McCullough Creek. However, the grassy bottom of it was almost always moist, and in some wet years enough water was in it to even count as flowing, although neither of us ever thought of it as a stream. Mostly it was good for grouse, along the grassy edges. And there were woodcock in the dogwood and hazel on the gentle slopes on each side.

As woodcock cover, the woods deteriorated in later years to the point where we rarely hunted it. From all appearances, neither did other hunters, except early in the season for grouse. Once in a while, Roy and I worked through it mostly for old times' sake, usually late in the grouse season, long after the woodcock had gone, often after the early winter's snow had covered the upland woods and grassy swales.

It was on one of these late-season grouse hunts, following two or three years of absence, that Roy and I found the beaver pond.

It was frozen, of course. Not such that we could walk out on it (I'm scared of frozen ponds in late fall), and I tried to keep Speck back too. But there was no open water, and little windblown drifts of snow made diagonal white stripes across the otherwise black ice.

We were astonished at first at the very presence of the pond, for we had never seen one before anywhere in McCullough's woods. It took us a little while to realize that this was the long, diagonal dry run, tributary to the creek, that now must have a new beaver dam at its downstream end.

There was not much snow on the ground that day, and Roy and I and Speck made our way down one edge of the pond.

One grouse flushed wild, way ahead, from the brushy edge, and flew across the ice and out of sight. That's all we saw, but we wanted to get down all the way to the dam. We did, and, standing on the long dike of yellow, stripped aspen poles and brush that constituted the dam, we could look back up the pond's long expanse.

We saw the lodge about a hundred feet from the dam, a huge conical pile of logs and brush projecting up through the ice; we mused on the family of *Castor canadensis* that undoubtedly now was warm and dry in its interior. But beyond the lodge, spreading back to where we had just come from, was the long expanse of what had once been a grassy, brushy gully, stretching back into the woods that we had once known so well, and which now seemed so strange.

The most noticeable change to the pond and its basin was that the beavers had created a greater opening. For, in addition to the area of ice now, it was obvious that the total water area had recently been much larger. Trees and saplings had been killed, well back from the present sheet of ice. Smaller plants, alder, and other brush had already started in the riparian flats that lay parallel to the pond's edges. Most significantly, the beavers had done a fine job of thinning out the larger trees on both sides, and in their place were coming along dogwood, alder, and aspen suckers, brittle and leafless now in early winter: a clearing stretching for at least a quarter mile, a hundred yards wide.

It was natural succession starting over.

This was woodcock cover being built—in its younger stages now, but a covert that was destined to last for a decade, giving Roy and me and Danny, and Speck, some of our very best 'doodle days.

Roy and I moved to leave the dam. With a rubberized foot, I kicked the snow off a small log for better footing.

"We've got to come back for this," Roy said, with a last glance up the length of the frozen pond.

"We will," I replied. "Come October."

Come October, we did. We'd stopped to visit young McCullough at the farmhouse, and he'd said "Yes, there's been some woodcock there lately." And "No, I haven't heard any shooting in there." So we thanked him, promised to see him later in the day, and started off across the open field back of the barn. Speck trotted ahead.

Weatherwise, it was a quiet, nondescript day. Cloudy, windless, the air heavy, hinting at moisture to come later.

But the woods were colorful nevertheless, even without the sun. It was that time in early October when the leaves of the red maple were just starting to fall, but some birch leaves were still green. The colors were rich and saturated, and of course the foliage was still thick for good shooting throughout most of the eighty. But when we reached the upper end of the beaver pond, the woods with all their color fell back on each side, to leave the broad opening stretching far away toward the creek. There was plenty of shooting room.

It had been a bit of a dry summer, but the pond was brimful; apparently the beavers had been efficient and successful in their attempts to retain available water.

We started along the right side. I was by the water, Roy on my right up a little, in low brush.

And almost immediately Speck tightened up, birdy, and then stopped, Roy just behind her. He took another step, and a woodcock bolted up and flew straight down the side of the pond, in the open over the brush. Roy dropped it easily, and I sent Speck ahead for it.

Then, at my feet, another bird fluttered up and wheeled over the pond's surface. I held my shot, for it would have fallen into the water or on the other side. If hit, that is. Speck came back with Roy's bird.

In the next hundred yards, three more woodcock were raised, and Roy got another.

And then Speck began to work strangely, ahead

of me along the water's edge. "Maybe grouse!" I called
to Roy, but still it didn't look like grouse cover, and
Speck's actions somehow did not suggest either grouse
or woodcock. She was, well, too *tentative*.

The thought struck me just a flash of a second
before it happened. Fleeting, silent, swift—three dark
forms wheeled ghost-like up from the water's edge
twenty yards ahead. Snipe!

The first shot of my twenty-gauge dropped one;
my second missed, and I had no double. Then, two
more birds—my gun empty—and Roy dropped one.
Both fell into water, but not far from the edge, and
after some coaxing, Speck got them both. But she
didn't like them—neither the water nor the snipe.

Close relative to the woodcock, the Wilson's, or
jack, snipe, retains more of the shorebird traits than
the timberdoodle and is always near water. In the
eastern part of our state, woodland pools are ideal.
Darker, sleeker, lighter-weight, but still resembling a
woodcock, my first snipe as a boy had fooled me into
thinking I had shot a young, skinny, and off-color
woodcock. Their silent, wild flush and wheeling flight
never fails to impress me. I think they taste pretty
much like woodcock, and Roy and I have enjoyed more
than a few around our campfires.

There really weren't many woodcock around the
beaver pond that day. We only shot one more, on the
other side on the way back.

But two grouse had taken that occasion to
explore the blackberry around one end of the dam,

and there Speck made one of her best grouse points. It was the highlight of the day when two birds thundered out together, Roy took one and I the other, and both crashed into the pond-side brush simultaneously.

And we shot another snipe. Our campfire fare that night was deliciously diverse.

Later the same year, we went back. Two days in a row in mid-October, when the flight was down, we each came away from the pond with a brace of woodcock bulging our pockets. The young dogwood along those slopes seemed filled with birds. Even later in the season, the first week in November, when other coverts had been deserted by the southern departure of the migration, the beaver pond slopes held a few more birds. Right up to the last day of the season, when a skim of ice lay on the pond surface in the morning.

For ten years, McCullough's beaver pond cover produced some of our best woodcock hunting, mixed with a few grouse, and many snipe, too. In the early October days we always looked forward to snipe there, and were never disappointed. Some years were better than others, but even in dry autumns, the moist edges of the pond always attracted a few woodcock.

Then one year, Roy and I went into McCullough's woods in the early season, September, to find the beaver pond gone. We found a couple of woodcock along the slopes, one grouse at a grassy edge. But the pond basin was empty of water, and instead thick marsh grass covered the bottom, already yellow and dry. We hunted all around it that day, crossing the old dam, now silent of its former rush of water.

For some reason we were never able to perceive, the beavers had suddenly deserted their dam, lodge, and pond. Maybe the surrounding aspens had been cut to their idea of exhaustion. Maybe there had been too many dry years. But gone they were, and as far as we ever knew, they didn't come back again.

Roy and I still go back though, once in a while. But it's more like it was before the pond years—like a long, grassy slough, the woods closing in again from both sides.

But we'll not forget that long expanse of black water in the woods and sloping sides of dogwood and aspen saplings bursting with woodcock every mid-October—and silent, wheeling snipe.

For ten splendid years, *Castor canadensis* had given us one of our greatest hidden coverts.

CHAPTER 18

THE GLORY SEASON

OME years it happens, but not always. And don't ask me why, because I really haven't got it figured yet.

The Spanish gold, that is.

Of course, almost every year about the first week of September red maples appear flaming on south-facing slopes, and about the same time the black ash turns lemon-yellow in the swamps. Most years, though, the Spanish gold eludes me.

That the lure of woodcock hunting is sharpened

by autumn-colored coverts I have long known. Even woodcock feathers turn orange against the sky.

I don't feel the same about grouse. That comes later. After the foliage is down, when seeing and shooting are clearer. When the November sky is gray and windy and the first flurries whirl around the spruces at the edge of Elmer Olson's marsh, when the forest floor is brown and gray along the Blackrock, and the pothole headwater of the Little Popple is noisy with wind in the dry blades, and the alder and dogwood are barren and cold. Then is the time for grouse, for me. The rattle of wings climbing through bare and brittle branches matches then the harshness of approaching winter. Then I love grouse tracks in the snow—and a roasting bird in a wood range oven on a freezing afternoon.

But the cold and snow are not for woodcock. The timberdoodle runs from the spectres of storm and freezing earth like a sandpiper from a crashing wave on a sandy beach—only to return in the warm promise of springtime, like the sandpiper when the wave recedes.

No, not the cold silence of winter for him. The woodcock is a player on a more dynamic stage. For, as autumn leaves turn and fall, so does the woodcock descend from his northern coverts. He starts to move when the leaves of the red maple and black ash first fall to ground. And he accelerates his southward migration as the sugar maples color to their own diversity, as the birch and aspens gradually change their fashion from green to gold.

For the timberdoodle—and for those who love and hunt him—this is the *glory season.*

Almost suddenly the season is late.

It doesn't always happen, not every year. Only when the fall weather has been just right for some reason—when it's only the aspens that still hold their yellow leaves—perhaps only when a late afternoon sun emblazons the sky with an eye-burning blue.

Only then, as the northern breezes stop stock-still for a few lingering hours, or moments, then might the aspen's earthly yellow turn to the ancient splendor of *Spanish gold.*

Not everyone can see it, of course, this last gilding of the glory season.

Maybe just woodcock hunters.

Roy was quiet, pensive. Inside the old iron stove a chunk of wood fell, and there was the sound of sparks, at which Speck perked up suddenly from her rug. Outside a cold rain dribbled on the roof of the "Whistle and Drum." It was late October.

We had come up the day before, and the weather had gone from threatening to worse. From the log tie that spanned the shack's interior now hung a diversity of pants, shirts, socks, and long johns, drying in the heat of the stove underneath. We had the Coleman lantern lighted, although it was only mid-afternoon. Yesterday the grouse, at least, had been cooperative, and we had two birds cut up and ready for the stew pot. All told, in the two days, we had put up just one woodcock, also yesterday. And we missed that, I had reminded Roy a few minutes ago.

"Good thing," he said.

Today we had hunted little, just enough to get wet again, and saw no birds.

But the season had been good to us.

We reminisced.

The Little Popple covert, behind the shack, had given us at least a half-dozen woodcock, including our first and our last of the season. Elmer Olson's marsh, a good dozen. The cover east of Poppletown, at the height of the migration, for three days running literally exploded with woodcock. Through the season at the "Whistle and Drum" we had broiled woodcock *hors d'oeuvres,* roast woodcock with dressing for our supper entrée, woodcock stew for lunch, woodcock with rice, with mushroom soup and noodles, and in white gravy on biscuits for breakfast.

For brilliant dog work, one day along the Blackrock stands out. It was still early in the season—mid-September—when Roy and Danny and I drove up to the family cabin for a weekend. Speck was with us. The valley slopes and floodplains along the river were a riot of yellow and crimson, too much foliage, really, for good shooting.

But the day was cool and sunny, the birds plentiful, and the smell of gunsmoke was satisfying, even if our game pockets were light.

By the time we had worked upstream to the mouth of Little Cat Creek, one hour, we had expended a dozen shells, and Roy had collected one woodcock.

Near the mouth of the creek, in a delta pointed into the corner between the two streams, was a patch of dogwood and blackberry, occupying about a two-acre flat bench perched above the river. It was usually good for two or three birds, but thick and hard to hunt. It was here, in fact, where Danny had shot his first woodcock, a half-dozen years ago.

We had walked into it, three abreast, and though it was thick with early-season foliage, we stayed in sight of each other. I was in the middle, Speck in front of me by forty feet. And just as she disappeared, her bell stopped.

"Point!" I yelled, and stepped forward.

I heard a rush of wings. I saw one bird clear the tops of the dogwood, and I shot, in the clear. And as the bird dropped, two more got up to my left. I missed with my second barrel, and then more wings to my left!

There, Danny's gun barked once, but I couldn't see what happened.

More wings whistled now to my right. Roy's gun sounded twice, then Danny's again. And I lost track. And then it was quiet.

The gunsmoke and feathers drifted away. Danny let loose an epithet. "Good Heavens!" Roy mimicked.

"What's the damages?" I shouted. "I got one."

"I got one," from Roy.

"I got two," from Danny. "I think."

"We'll never find 'em," Roy offered. "Not in this cover."

"Stand still and let Speck give them a try."

I couldn't see her, nor hear her, but I thought she was not far ahead in the dogwood.

"Fetch!" I said, not loudly, and her bell jingled.

In another minute, she jingled back and neatly placed a woodcock in my hand.

Three more times I ordered "Fetch!" and three more times, one by one, Speck went out and, one by one, she came back in with a bird, the last one still alive and able to walk. She caught it again. And then she sat down and looked me in the eye. I went down on one knee, to embrace her, and my cup ran over.

A week later Roy and I were up on the West Branch of the Mooselick, with tent, to finish out the trout season and also try for birds. We were away five days and had four suppers in camp. One supper was all trout, one all woodcock, one of grouse, and one of all three. The hamburger we'd brought along, for an emergency supper of spaghetti, we gave to Speck.

By mid-October, the timberdoodle migration was in full swing. Fall leaves were mostly gone around the cabin on the Blackrock, so in addition to plentiful woodcock, we picked up a grouse here and there along the river. In rapid succession, we hunted the Alder Creek Chapel cover and the School Trust Forty (both of which were now getting too grown up). But one day the slough that had once held McCullough's beaver pond gave us three woodcock and a grouse.

Glory season, indeed.

When we came up to the "Whistle and Drum" yesterday morning, the sky was only cloudy. But it was windy, and here and there in the woods a shower of yellow aspen leaves would whip down around us from high overhead. Moments of sunlight broke through, but it was obvious that the weather was changing.

We pounded the coverts hard around the shack, the Little Popple, part of Elmer Olson's marsh, and others, all day. I don't remember where we saw—and missed—the one woodcock. One of the grouse made the mistake of holding too long and flushing out from under my feet at the edge of the marsh.

In late afternoon, the wind dropped nearly to a dead calm. And in that stillness, by the rock pile at the edge of the old field clearing, Speck pointed the second grouse. Roy dropped it cleanly in the open, and Speck retrieved it with a flourish—to Roy.

Little color remained in the old field—only the dark green of spruces nearing twenty feet tall and, against their shadow, the orange flags of blackberry. But as we turned to recross the clearing and head for the shack, the clouds thinned overhead, and the clearing was quickly warmed in the light of a sudden sun. The blackberry leaves sparkled.

And then it was I saw it, for the first time this fall. A clump of aspens, in the far northeast corner of the clearing, stood tall with most of their foliage. And in that late afternoon sun, against a deep blue of northern sky, the aspens' *Spanish gold* shone stark and brilliant.

Transfixed, Roy and I watched it for a full couple of minutes, not speaking, and Speck was quiet at our feet. But the clouds thickened again overhead, and the sun was put out. A gust of wind stirred.

We turned away in shadow, toward the darkening western sky, toward the "Whistle and Drum."

Behind us, a few golden coins showered from the tallest aspen.

Roy tossed another chunk of birch into the iron stove, stood up to our kitchen shelf along one wall, and started in on the stew. I picked up and rinsed our coffee cups, and then reached for the cooler. It was nearly dark now outside the windows.

That night it froze, hard. The drizzle had turned to snow in the night, and now the clearing around the shack was dusted with white. It was pretty, in its way, especially now with no wind and a brilliant but cold sun. No clouds marred the morning sky. We were due to leave for home at noon.

"Let's work up and around to the old field clearing again," I suggested to Roy. "At least there was a grouse there a couple days ago."

"That will just about take up our morning," Roy said. "Let's do it."

Of course, it was not really the field clearing grouse we wanted to check out. What I really was anxious to see was whether those aspen branches were really bare now, and I thought they might be.

It did take us just about the morning to work our way up to the clearing—around part of Olson's marsh (where we flushed one grouse but didn't get a shot), east of our eighty and into our neighbor's pasture, north along the fence row, back west through a couple of our smaller clearings, and then to the rock pile. No more grouse. And no woodcock.

Arriving within sight of the aspens, it was plain that all branches were bare, and we couldn't even be sure which were the ones we sought. But when closer, then of course we could tell. For, scattered on the ground covering nearly an acre, we guessed, were strewn thousands of yellow coins, briefly irradiated now by the mid-day sun against the gray and brown of autumn earth. No longer gold, and soon to be just dead and decomposing aspen leaves.

We turned away.

And I knew, as always, that when the last coins of Spanish gold had fallen, the last of the season's woodcock would be gone, too.

LEGACY

s soon as Speck tightened into a point at the base of a hazel clump, I stepped back in some alders, keeping a branch out of my face. Beside me now was a new hunting partner, aged thirteen. Farther over to the right a little, Danny had stopped, too, watchful.

"What do I do now?" Ben asked.

He had had a fair amount of practice on hand-thrown targets and had gotten the hang of it a full year ago. He had powdered many of the clay birds.

Now he stood transfixed, his undersized single twenty gauge half-raised, eyes frozen to the dog.

"Step up behind her," I said. "Right up beside her."

I held my breath. It was the ancient moment, so old, and yet so new and heart stopping each time. To Ben, so very new. He took another step beside Speck.

The big, brown butterfly fluttered up from the hazel, leveled, rocketed off to the right. My stomach felt somewhere about midpoint of my larynx.

The little twenty gauge flashed to his shoulder, swung to the right, barked once. Hey, smooth! I thought. Real smooth!

The woodcock hurtled on, banked in front of the woods at the pasture's edge, morning sunlight glinting off its flashing wings. It wheeled over a low mound of willows, and disappeared. My stomach began to fall back into place.

Ben turned around, his lips drawn tight. He looked like I felt.

"I missed him." Quietly, not angry, no tears. My heartbeat slowed down, near normal.

"Yep," I replied. "You sure did."

I remembered another alder thicket, at the edge of an autumn-colored woods, another big, brown butterfly that had burst in front of young eyes, so long ago. Silently and secretly, a glow of understanding came across my consciousness, like a sudden wind rushing against the morning fog along the Blackrock.

With the wisdom of years (I thought), I knew it

was better to miss the first one.

"Are there more up ahead?" Ben asked, his young voice breaking my reverie.

I looked over at Danny. He stood with gun still hanging over his elbow, watching the little drama, a grin starting to twitch at the corner of his mouth. I grinned back.

"Yes, Ben," I answered, "there's more up ahead." I drew in a deep breath, cleared my throat. "Many more."

He turned back to face the low sun coming through the hazel and alder.

"Then let's go."

Speck was fussing at our feet; she nosed into the hazel clump once more, then at my side.

"Hup, Speck," I said. "This here young Ben of ours is after his first woodcock today. He says let's go."

Ben looked up at me, and laughed. I chuckled back.

Speck padded across our track, wheeled in front of Ben, and then trotted ahead into the pasture.

E N D